Charlotte Mary Yonge

Love and life;

An old story in eighteenth century costume - Vol. 2

Charlotte Mary Yonge

Love and life;
An old story in eighteenth century costume - Vol. 2

ISBN/EAN: 9783337872595

Printed in Europe, USA, Canada, Australia, Japan

Cover: Foto ©ninafisch / pixelio.de

More available books at **www.hansebooks.com**

LOVE AND LIFE

AN

Old Story in Eighteenth Century Costume

LOVE AND LIFE

AN

Old Story in Eighteenth Century Costume

BY

CHARLOTTE M. YONGE

AUTHOR OF THE "HEIR OF REDCLYFFE," ETC., ETC.

IN TWO VOLUMES

VOLUME II

London

MACMILLAN AND CO.

1880

CONTENTS.

CHAPTER I.
	PAGE
THE MUFFLED BRIDEGROOM	1

CHAPTER II.
THE SISTERS' MEETING	15

CHAPTER III.
A FATAL SPARK	47

CHAPTER IV.
WEALTH AND DESOLATION	56

CHAPTER V.
THE WANDERER	63

CHAPTER VI.
VANISHED	81

CONTENTS.

CHAPTER VII.
THE TRACES 101

CHAPTER VIII.
CYTHEREA'S BOWER 116

CHAPTER IX.
THE ROUT 135

CHAPTER X.
A BLACK BLONDEL 152

CHAPTER XI.
THE FIRST TASK 169

CHAPTER XII.
THE SECOND TASK 196

CHAPTER XIII.
LIONS 210

CHAPTER XIV.
THE COSMETIC 225

CHAPTER XV.

DOWN THE RIVER 241

CHAPTER XVI.

THE RETURN 255

CHAPTER XVII.

WAKING 269

CHAPTER XVIII.

MAKING THE BEST OF IT 291

LOVE AND LIFE:

AN

Old Story in Eighteenth Century Costume.

CHAPTER I.

THE MUFFLED BRIDEGROOM.

This old fantastical Duke of dark corners.—
Measure for Measure

THERE was some coming and going of Mr. Hargrave in the ensuing weeks; and it began to be known that Miss Delavie was to become the wife of the recluse. Mrs. Aylward evidently knew it, but said nothing; Molly preferred a petition to be her waiting maid; Jumbo grinned as if overpowered with inward mirth; the old ladies in the pew looked more sour and haughty than ever to discourage "the artful minx," and the little girls asked all manner of absurd and puzzling questions.

My Lady was still at Bath, and Aurelia supposed that the marriage would take place on her return; and that the Major and Betty would perhaps accompany her. The former was quite in his usual health again, and had himself written to give her his blessing as a good dutiful maiden, and declare that he hoped to be with her for her wedding, and to give her himself to his honoured friend.

She was the more amazed and startled when, one Sunday evening in spring, Mr. Hargrave came to her as she sat in her own parlour, saying, "Madam, you will be amazed, but under the circumstances, the parson and myself being both here, Mr. Belamour trusts you will not object to the immediate performance of the ceremony."

Aurelia took some moments to realise what the ceremony was; and then she cried, "Oh! but my father meant to have been here."

"Mr. Belamour thinks it better not to trouble Major Delavie to come up," said Mr. Hargrave;

and as Aurelia stood in great distress and disappointment at this disregard of her wishes, he added, "I think Miss Delavie cannot fail to understand Mr. Belamour's wishes to anticipate my Lady's arrival, so that he may be as little harassed as possible with display and publicity. You may rely both on his honour and my vigilance that all is done securely and legally."

"Oh! I know that," said Aurelia, blushing; "but it is so sudden! And I was thinking of my father——"

"Your honoured father has given full consent in writing," said the steward. "Your doubts and scruples are most natural, my dear madam, but under the circumstances they must give way, for it would be impossible to Mr. Belamour to go through a public wedding."

That Aurelia well knew, though she had expected nothing so sudden or so private; but she began to feel that she must allow all to be as he chose; and she remembered that she had never pressed on him her longing for her father's presence, having taken it as a matter of course, and which a public wedding was sure to be attended. Every one knew of excellent and respectable couples who had not been known to be married till the knot had been tied for several days or weeks—so that there was nothing in this to shock the bride. And as usual she did as she was told, and let Mr. Hargrave lead her by her finger-tips towards Mr. Belamour's apartments. Mrs. Aylward was waiting in the lobby, with a fixed impassive countenance, intended to imply that though obedient to the summons to serve as a witness, it was no concern of hers. On the stairs behind her the maids were leaning over the balusters, stuffing their aprons into their mouths lest their tittering should betray them.

The sitting-room was nearly, but not quite, dark, for a lamp, closely shaded, cast a dim light on a Prayer-book, placed on a small table, behind which stood poor Mr. Greaves—a black spectre, whose white bands were just discernible below a face whose nervous, disturbed expression was lost in the general gloom. He carefully avoided looking at the bride, fearing perhaps besides, having been far too shy to enter on the subject of her wedding. So she rose up as in a dream, saying, "Shall I go as I am?"

"I fear a fuller toilet would be lost upon the bridegroom," said the lawyer with some commiseration, as he looked at the beautiful young creature about to be bound to the heart-broken old hermit. "You will have to do me the honour of accepting my services in the part of father."

He was a man much attached to the family, and especially to Mr. Belamour, his first patron, and was ready to do anything at his bidding or for his pleasure. Such private weddings were by no means uncommon up to the middle of the last century. The State Law was so easy as to render Gretna Green unnecessary, when the presence of any clergyman anywhere, while the parties plighted their troth before witnesses, was sufficient to legalise the union; nor did any shame or sense of wrong necessarily attach to such marriages. Indeed they were often the resource of persons too bashful or too refined to endure the display and boisterous merriment by some appeal on her part such as would make his situation perplexing. Contempt and poverty had brought his stamp of clergymen very low, and rendered them abject. He had been taken by surprise, and though assured that this was according to my Lady's will, and with the consent of the maiden's father, he was in an agony of fright, shifting awkwardly from leg to leg, and ruffling the leaves of the book, as a door opened and the bridegroom appeared, followed by Jumbo.

Aurelia looked up with bashful eagerness, and saw in the imperfect light a tall figure entirely covered by a long dark dressing-gown, a grey, tight curled lawyer's wig on the head, and the upper part of the face sheltered from the scanty rays of the lamp by a large green shade.

Taking his place opposite to her as Mr. Hargrave arranged them, he bowed in silence to the clergyman, who, in a trembling voice, began the rite which was to unite Amyas Belamour to Aurelia Delavie. He intended to shorten the service, but his nervous terror and the obscurity of the room made him stumble in finding the essential passages, and blunder in dictating the vows, thus increasing the confusion and bewilderment of poor little Aurelia. Somehow her one comfort was in the touch of the hand that either clasped hers, or held the ring on her finger—a strong, warm, tender, trustworthy hand, neither as white nor as soft as she would have expected, but giving her a comfortable sense both of present support and affection, and of identity with that eager one which had sought to fondle and caress her. There was a certain tremor about both, but hers was from bashful fright, his, from scarcely suppressed eagerness.

The steward had a form of certificate ready for signature. When it was presented to the bridegroom he put up his hand for a moment as if to push back the shade, but, in dread of admitting even a feeble ray of light, gave up the attempt, took the pen, and wrote Amyas Belamour where the clergyman pointed. Aurelia could hardly see what she was doing, and knew she had written very badly. The lawyer and housekeeper followed as witnesses; and the bridegroom, laying a fee of ten guineas on the desk, took his bride by the hand and led her within the door whence he had issued. It was instantly closed, and at the same moment she was enfolded in a pair of rapturous arms, and held to a breast whose throbs wakened response in her own, while passionate kisses rained on her face, mingled with ecstatic whispers and murmurs of " Mine! mine! my own!"

On a knock at the door she was hastily released, and Mr. Hargrave said, " Here are the certificates, sir."—Mr. Belamour put one into her hand, saying, "Keep it always about you; never part with it. And now, my child, after all the excitement you have gone through, you shall be subjected to no more to-night. Fare you well, and blessings attend your dreams."

Strange that while he was uttering this almost peremptory dismissal, she should feel herself in a clinging grasp, most unwilling to let her go! What did it all mean? Could she indeed be a wife, when here she was alone treading the long dark stair, in looks, in habits, in externals, still only the little governess of my Lady's children!

However, she had hardly reached her room, before there was a knock at the door, and the giggling, blushing entrance of Molly with " Please ma'am, Madam Belamour, I wishes you joy with all my heart. Please can't I do nothing for you? Shall I help you undress, or brush your hair?"

Perhaps she expected a largesse in honour of the occasion, but Aurelia had spent all her money on Christmas gifts, and had nothing to bestow. However, she found on the breakfast-table a parcel addressed to Madam Belamour, containing a purse with a startling amount of golden guineas in it. She was rather surprised at the title, which was one generally conferred on dignified matrons whose husbands were below the rank of knighthood, such as the wives of country squires and of the higher clergy. The calling her mother Madam Delavie had been treated as an offence by Lady Belamour; and when the day had gone by, with nothing else to mark it from others, Aurelia, finding her recluse in what she mentally called his quiet rational mood, ventured, after thanking him, modestly to inquire whether that was what she was to be called.

"It is better thus," he said. "You have every right to the title."

She recollected that he was a baronet's younger son, a distinction in those days; and that she had been told that his patent of knighthood had been made out, though he had never been able to appear at court to receive the accolade, and had never assumed the title; so she only said "Very well, sir, I merely thought whether my Lady would think it presuming."

He laughed a little. "My Lady will soon understand it," he said. "Her husband will be at home in a few weeks. And now, my dear Madam Belamour," he added, playfully, "tell me whether there is any wish that I can gratify."

"You are very kind, sir——"

"What does that pause mean, my fair friend?"

"I fear it is too much to ask, sir, but since you inquire what would please me most, it would be if you could spare me to go to my sister Harriet's wedding?"

"My child," he said, with evident regret, "I fear that cannot be. It will not be prudent to make any move until Mr. Wayland's return; but after that I can assure you of more liberty. Meantime, let us consider what wedding present you would like to send her."

Aurelia had felt her request so audacious that she subsided easily; and modestly suggested a tea-service. She thought of porcelain, but Mr. Belamour's views were of silver, and it ended in the lady giving the cups and saucers, and the gentleman the urn and the tea and coffee pots and other plate; but it was a drawback to the pleasure of this munificence that the execution of the order had to be entrusted to Mr. Hargrave. The daring hope Aurelia had entertained of shopping for a day, with Mrs. Aylward as an escort, and choosing the last fashions to send to her sisters, was quashed by the grave reply that it was better not for the present. What was the meaning of all this mystery, and when was it to end? She felt that it would be ungrateful to murmur, for Mr. Belamour evidently was full of sorrow whenever he was obliged to disappoint her, and much was done for her pleasure. A charming little saddle-horse, two riding-habits, with a groom, and a horse for him, were sent down from London for her benefit; gifts showered upon her; and whenever she found her husband in one of those perplexing accesses of tenderness she was sure to carry away some wonderful present, a beautiful jewelled watch, an *etui* case, a fan, a scent-bottle, or patch-box with a charming enamel of a butterfly. The little girls were always looking for something pretty that she would show them in the morning, and thought it must be a fine thing to have a husband who gave such charming things. Those caressing evenings, however, always frightened Aurelia, and sent her away vaguely uneasy, often to lie awake full of a vague yearning and alarm; and several days of restlessness would pass before she could return to her ordinary enjoyment of her days with the children and her evenings with Mr. Belamour. Yet when there was any long intermission of those fits of tender affection, she missed them sorely, and began to fear she had given offence, especially as this strangely capricious man seemed sometimes to repel those modest, timid advances which at other times would fill him with ill-suppressed transport. Then came longings to see and satisfy herself as to what was indeed the aspect of him whom she was learning to love.

No wonder there was something unsettled and distressed about her, overthrowing much of that gentle duteousness which she had brought from home. She wrote but briefly and scantily to her sister, not feeling as if she could give full confidence; she drifted away from some of the good habits enjoined on her, feeling that, as a married woman, she was less under authority. She was less thorough in her religious ways, less scrupulous in attending to the children's lessons; and the general fret of her uncertainties told upon her temper with them. They loved her heartily still, and she returned their affection, but she was not so uniformly patient and good-humoured. Indeed since Amoret's departure some element of harmony was missing, and it could not now be said that a whine, a quarrel, or a cry was a rare event Even the giving up my Lady's wearisome piece of embroidery had scarcely a happy effect, for Aurelia missed the bracing of the task-work and the attention it required, and the unoccupied time was spent in idle fretting. A little self-consequence too began to set in, longing for further recognition of the dignities of Madam Belamour.

The marriage had been notified to Lady Belamour and to Major Delavie, and letters had been received from each. My Lady travelled to London early in April in company with Lady Aresfield, and, to the relief of the inmates of Bowstead, made no deviation thither. No one else was officially told that the wedding had taken place, but all the village knew it; and Mrs. Phœbe and Mrs. Delia so resented it that they abandoned the state pew to Madam Belamour and the children, made their curtsies more perpendicularly than ever, and, when formally invited to supper, sent a pointed and ceremonious refusal, so that Aurelia felt hurt and angered.

CHAPTER II.

THE SISTERS' MEETING.

> By all the hope thou hast to see again
> Our aged father and to soothe his pain,
> I charge thee, tell me, hast thou seen the thing
> Thou callst thine husband?—MORRIS.

AFTER numerous delays Mr. Arden had at length been presented to the living of Rundell Canonicorum, and in one of the last days of April Harriet Delavie had become his wife. After a fortnight of festivities amongst their old Carminster friends, the happy couple were to ride, pillion-wise, to take possession of their new home, passing through London, and there spending time enough with some relations of the bridegroom to show Harriet the wonders of the City.

Thence Mrs. Arden sent an urgent invitation from her hospitable hostess to Mrs. Belamour, to come and spend some days in Gracechurch Street, and share with her sister the pleasures of the first sight of London.

"I assure you," wrote Harriet, "that though they be Woolstaplers, it is all in the Wholesale Line; and they are very genteel, and well-bred Persons, who have everything handsome about them. Indeed it is upon the Cards that the Alderman may, ere many years be passed, be my Lord Mayor; but yet he and his good Wife have a proper Appreciation of Family, and know how to esteem me as one of the Delavies. They would hold themselves infinitely honoured by your Visit; and if you were here, we might even be invited to Lady Belamour's, and get Tickets for Ranelagh. I called at my Lady's Door, but she was not within, nor has she returned my Visit, though I went in the Alderman's own Coach; but if you were with me she would have no Colour for Neglect, you being now her Sister-in-law, though it makes me laugh to think of it. But as we poor married Ladies are compelled to obey our Lords and Masters; and as

Mr. Belamour may chance to be too high in his Notions to permit you to be a Guest in this House (as I told our good Cousin Arden was very like), we intend to lie a Night at Brentford, and remain there for a Day, trusting that your Husband will not be so cruel as to prevent a Meeting, either by your coming to see us, or our coming to see you in your present Abode, which I long to do. It is a Year since we parted, and I cannot tell you how I long to clasp my beloved Sister in my Arms."

Harriet could not long more for such a meeting than did Aurelia, and there was, it must be owned, a little relief, that it was Harriet, and not the severer judge, Betty, who thus awaited her She could hardly brook the delay until the evening, and even wondered whether it were not a wife's privilege to anticipate the hour; but she did not venture, and only hovered about impatient for Jumbo's summons. She came in with a rapid movement that led Mr. Belamour to say, "Ha, my fair visitor, I perceive that you have some tidings to bring me to-day."

Everything was rapidly poured out, and she anxiously awaited the decision. She had little hope of being allowed to go to Gracechurch Street, and did not press for it; but she could not refrain from showing her earnest desire for the sight of her sister, so that it was plain that it would have been a cruel disappointment to her, if she had been prevented from meeting the newly-married couple. She detected a certain sound of annoyance or perplexity in the tones that replied, and her accents became almost plaintively imploring as she concluded, " Pray, pray, sir, do not deny me."

" No, my child, I could not be cruel enough for a refusal," he answered; " I was but considering how most safely the thing may be contrived. I know it would be your wish, and that it would seem more befitting that you should act as hostess to your sister, but I fear that must be for another time. This is not my house, and there are other reasons for which it would be wiser for you to receive no one here."

" It will be quite enough for me if I may only go to Brentford to meet my dear, dear Harriet."

THE SISTERS' MEETING.

"Then be it so, my child. Present my compliments to Mrs. Arden, and entreat her to excuse the seeming inhospitality of the invalid."

Aurelia was overflowing with joy at the anticipated meeting, wrote a delighted letter to make the appointment, and skipped about the dark stairs and passages more like the butterfly she was than like Madam Belamour; while Fay and Letty found her a more delightful playfellow than ever, recovering all the animation she had lost during the last weeks. Her only drawback to the pleasure was that each intervening evening convinced her more strongly that Mr. Belamour was uneasy and dissatisfied about the meeting, which he could not prohibit. On the previous night he asked many questions about her sister, in especial whether she were of an inquisitive disposition.

"That rather depends on how much she has to say about herself," returned Aurelia, after some reflection. "She likes to hear about other people's affairs, but she had much rather talk of her own."

This made Mr. Belamour laugh. "Considering," he said, "how recently she has undergone the greatest event of a woman's life, let us hope that her imagination and her tongue may be fully occupied by it during the few hours that you are to pass together. It seems hard to put any restraint on your ingenuous confidence, my sweet friend; but I trust to your discretion to say as little as you can contrive of your strange position here, and of the infirmities and caprices of him whose name you have deigned to bear."

"Sir, do you think I could?"

"It is not for my own sake, but for yours, that I would recommend caution," he continued. "The situation is unusual, and such disclosures might impel persons to interfere for what they thought your interest; but you have promised me your implicit trust, and you will, I hope, prove it. You can understand how painful would be such well-meaning interference, though you cannot understand how fatally mischievous it would be."

"I had better say I can tell her nothing," said Aurelia, startled.

"Nay, that would excite still greater suspicion. Reply briefly and carefully, making no mysteries to excite curiosity, and avert the conversation from yourself as much as possible."

Man of the world and brilliant talker as he had been, he had no notion of the difficulty of the task he had imposed on the simple openhearted girl, accustomed to share all her thoughts with her sister; and she was too gay and joyous to take full note of all his cautions, only replying sincerely that she hoped that she should say nothing amiss, and that she would do her best to be heedful of his wishes.

In spite of all such cautions, she was too happy to take in the notion of anxiety. She rose early in the morning, caring for the first time to array herself in the insignia of her new rank. Knowing that the bridle-path lay through parks, woodlands, and heaths, so that there was no fear of dust, she put on a dainty habit of white cloth, trimmed and faced with blue velvet, and a low-crowned hat with a white feather. On her pretty grey horse, the young Madam Belamour was a fair and gracious sight, as she rode into the yard of the Red Lion at Brentford. Harriet was at the window watching for her, and Mr. Arden received her as she sprang off her steed, then led her up to the parlour, where breakfast was spread awaiting her.

"Aurelia, what a sweet figure you make," cried Harriet, as the sisters unwound their arms after the first ecstasy of embracing one another again. "Where did you get that exquisite habit?"

"It came down from London with another, a dark blue," said Aurelia. "I suppose Mr. Belamour ordered them, for they came with my horse. It is the first time I have worn it."

"Ah! fine things are of little account when there is no one to see them," said Mrs. Arden, shaking her head in commiseration.

She was attired in a grey riding-dress with a little silver lace about it, and looked wonderfully plump and well, full of importance and complacency, and with such a return of comeliness that Aurelia would hardly have recognised the lean, haggard, fretful Harriet of the previous year. Her sentiment and romance, her soft melancholy and little affectations had departed, and she was already the notable prosperous wife of a beneficed clergyman, of whose abilities she was very proud, though she patronised with good-humoured contempt his dreamy, unpractical, unworldly ways.

The questions poured forth from Aurelia's heart-hunger about brother, sister and home, were answered kindly and fully over the breakfast-table; but as if Harriet had turned that page in her life, and expected Aurelia to have done the same, every now and then exclaiming: "La! you have not forgotten that! What a memory you have, child!"

She wanted much more to talk of the parsonage and glebe of Rundell Canonicorum, and of how many servants and cows she should keep, and showed herself almost annoyed when Aurelia brought her back to Carminster by asking whether Eugene had finished his Comenius, and if the speckled hen had hatched many chickens, whether Palmer had had his rheumatic attack this spring, or if the Major's letter to Vienna had produced any tidings of Nannerl's relations. Harriet seemed only to be able to reply by an effort of memory, and was far more desirous of expatiating on the luxuries at Alderman Arden's, and the deference with which she had been treated, in contrast to the indignity of Lady Belamour's neglect.

It was disappointing to find that her father had heard nothing from my Lady about the settlement of the Manor House.

"Was the promise in writing?" asked Mr. Arden, who had been silent all this time.

"Certainly, in a letter to me."

"I recommend you to keep it carefully until Mr. Wayland's return," said Mr. Arden: "he will see justice done to you."

"Poor Mr. Wayland! When he does return, I pity him; but it is his own fault for leaving his lady to herself. Have you ever seen the gallant Colonel, sister?"

"Never."

"Ah! most like he is not much at Bowstead. But do not folk talk there?"

"My dear," said Mr. Arden, "you would do well to imitate your honoured father's discretion on certain points."

"Bless me, Mr. Arden, how you startled me. I thought you were in a brown study." She winked at Aurelia as if to intimate that she meant to continue the subject in his absence, and went on: "I assure you, I had to be on the alert all the way to take care he looked at the sign-posts, or we might have been at York by this time. And in London, what do you think was all my gentleman cared to go and see? Why, he must needs go to some correspondents of his who are Fellows of the Royal Society. I took it for granted they must be friends of his Majesty or of the Prince of Wales at the least, and would have had him wait for his new gown and cassock; but la! it was only a set of old doctors and philosophers, and he wished to know what musty discoveries they had been making. That was one thing he desired in London, and the other was to hear that crazy Parson Wesley preach a sermon hours long!"

"I was well rewarded in both instances," said Mr. Arden gravely.

Aurelia did not take advantage of the opportunity of shining in the eyes of her new brother-in-law by showing her acquaintance with the discussions on electricity which she had studied for Mr. Belamour's benefit, nor did she speak of Dr. Godfrey's views of Wesley and Whitfield. Had she so ventured, her sister would have pitied her, and Mr. Arden himself been somewhat shocked at her being admitted to knowledge unbecoming to a pretty young lady. Intellect in ladies would have been a startling idea, and though very fond of his wife, he never thought of her as a companion, but only as the mistress of his house and guardian of his welfare.

The dinner was ordered at one, and at three Aurelia would ride home, while Mr. and Mrs. Arden went on about twelve miles to the house of a great grazier, brother to the Alderman's wife, where they had been invited to make their next stage, and spend the next day, Sunday, when Harriet reckoned on picking up information about cattle, if she were not actually presented with a cow or a calf. They went out and walked a little about the town, where presently they met Mrs. Hunter. Aurelia met her puzzled stare with a curtsey, and she shouted in her hearty tone "Miss Delavie!—I mean Mrs. Belamour! Who would have thought of seeing you here!"

"I am here to meet my sister—Mrs. Arden. Let me—let me present you," said Aurelia in obedience to an imperious sign from her sister, going through the form for the first time, while Harriet volubly declared her happiness in making Mrs. Hunter's acquaintance, and explained how they were on their way to take possession of Mr. Arden's rectory of Rundell Canonicorum, the words rolling out of her mouth with magnificent emphasis. "I congratulate you, ma'am," said Mrs. Hunter, cordially, "and you too, my dear," she added, turning to Aurelia. "I would have been out long ago to call on you—a sort of relation as you are now, as I may say—but it was kept all so mum, one never knew the time to drink your health; and my Cousins Treforth wouldn't so much as give me a hint. But la! says I, why should you talk about artfulness? I'm right glad poor Mr. Amyas should find a sprightly young lady to cure him of his mopishness.

"Never mind them, my dear, if they do look sour on you. I'll come over one of these days and talk to them. Now, I must have you come in to take your dinner with us. The Doctor will be right pleased to find you. I'll take no excuse. I thank Heaven I'm always ready whoever may drop in. There's spring chicken and sparrow-grass."

However, on hearing their dinner was ordered at the inn, the good lady was satisfied that to dine with her was impossible; but she insisted on their coming in to partake of wine and cake in her best parlour.

This, however, was a little more than Mr. Arden could endure, he made an excuse about seeing to the horse, and escaped; while Mrs. Hunter led the two sisters to her closely shut-up parlour, wainscoted, and hung with two staring simpering portraits of herself and her husband, clean as soap could make it, but smelling like a long closed box. She went to a cupboard in the wall, and brought out a silver salver, a rich cake, glasses and wine, and pouring out the wine, touched the glass with her lips, as she wished health and happiness to the two brides before her.

"We shall soon have another wedding in the family, if report speaks true," she added. "They say—but you should be the best informed, Madam Belamour—"

"We hear nothing of the matter, ma'am," said Aurelia.

"That's odd, since Mr. Belamour is young Sir Amyas's guardian; and they cannot well pass him over now he has begun life again as it were," laughed Mrs. Hunter. "'Tis said that my Lady is resolved the wedding shall be within six weeks."

"There are two words to that question," said Harriet, oracularly; "I know from good authority that young Sir Amyas is determined against the match."

"But is it true, ma'am," cried Mrs. Hunter, eagerly, "that my Lady and the Countess of Aresfield met at Bath, and that my Lady is to have 3,000*l.* down to pay off her debts before her husband comes home, the day her son is married to Lady Arabella?"

"Every word of it is true, ma'am," said Harriet, importantly.

"Well now, that folk should sell their own flesh and blood!"

"How have you heard it, sister Harriet?" asked Aurelia.

"From a sure hand, my love. No other than Mrs. Dove. She is wife to my Lady's coachman," explained Mrs. Arden to her hostess, "and nurse to the two children it is her pleasure to keep with her."

"Dear good Nurse Dove!" cried Aurelia, "did she come to see you?"

"Yes, that did she! So I have it from the fountain-head, as I may say, that the poor young gentleman's hand and heart are to be made over without his own will, that so his mother may not have such a schedule of debts wherewith to face her husband on his return!"

"Her jewels have been all paste long ago, I know very well," said Mrs. Hunter, not to be outdone; "though, would you believe it, Doctor Hunter is like all the men, and will believe nothing against her! But this beats all the rest! Why, I have it from my maid, who is sister to one of the servants at the boarding-school in Queen Square, whither they have sent the Lady Belle, that she is a regular little shrew. She flew at one of the other young ladies like a wild cat, because she did not yield place to her at once, and scratched her cheeks till the blood ran down, and tore out whole handfuls of her hair. She was like one possessed, and they had to call the lackey before they could get her safe tied down in bed, where they kept her on bread and water, trying to get her to make her apology; but not a word could be got out of her, till they had to yield the point lest she should fall sick."

Aurelia mentally applauded her own discretion in not capping this with Mrs. Dove's former tale, and only observing that the marriage could not take place before the young baronet was of age, without the consent of his personal guardian, Mr. Belamour.

"You will excuse me, my dear, in speaking of your husband, but he has so long been incapable of acting, that they say his consent can be dispensed with."

"Aye, poor cousin Amyas Belamour!" said Mrs. Hunter. "He was the only man who ever durst resist my Lady's will before, and you see to what she has brought him!"

"Her son is resisting her now," said Harriet; "and our good Dove says it makes her blood boil to see the way the poor young gentleman is treated. He, who was the darling for whom nothing was good enough a while ago, has now scarce a place in his mother's own house. She is cold and stately with him, and Colonel Mar, the Lady Belle's brother, being his commanding officer, there is no end to the vexations and annoyances they give him, both at home and in his quarters. Mrs. Dove says his own man, Grey, tells her it is a wonder how he stands out against it all! And a truly well-bred young gentleman he is. He came to pay me his call in Gracechurch Street only yesterday, knowing our kindred, and most unfortunate was it that I was stepped out to the office to speak as to our boxes being duly sent by the

Buckingham wain; but he left his ticket, and a message with the servant, 'Tell my cousin, Mrs. Arden, he said, 'that I much regret not having seen her, and I should have done myself the honour of calling sooner to inquire for her good father, if I had known she was in town.'"

"Well, I have never seen the young gentleman since he was a mere child," said Mrs. Hunter. "His mother has bred him to neglect his own home and relations, but I am sorry for him."

"They say," continued Harriet significantly, "that they are sure there is some cause for his holding out so stiffly—I verily believe my Lady suspected—"

"O hush, Harriet!" cried Aurelia, colouring painfully.

"Well, it is all over now, so you need not be offended," said Harriet, laughing. "Besides, if my Lady had any such notion when she brought about your marriage, she must be disappointed, for the young spark is as resolute as ever."

"And no wonder, if he knows what the lady is like," said Aurelia.

"Ah! he has admitted as much to the King."

"To the King!" cried both auditors.

"Oh yes! you know my Lady is very thick with my Lady Suffolk, and she persuaded the King to speak to him at the levée. '*Comment*,' says his majesty in French, 'are you a young rebel, sir, that refuse the good things your mother provides you?' Not a whit was my young gentleman moved. He bowed, and answered that he was acting by the desire of his guardian. Excuse me, sister, but the King answered—'A raving melancholic! That will not serve your turn, sir. Come to your senses, fulfil your mother's bond, and we'll put you on the Duke's staff, where you may see more of service than of home, or belike get into gay quarters, where you may follow any other *fantaisie* if that is making you commit such *bêtises!*' At that Sir Amyas, who is but an innocent youth, flamed up in his cheeks till they were as red as his coat, and said his honour was engaged; on which his majesty swore at him for an idiot, and turned his back. Every word of this Mrs. Dove heard Colonel Mar tell my Lady—and then they fell to rating the poor youth, and trying to force out who this secret flame may be; but he is of the same stuff as his mother, and as adamantine and impervious. And now the Colonel keeps him on hard duty continually, and they watch him day and night to find out what places he haunts. But bless me, Mrs. Hunter, is that the church clock striking? We must be gone, or my good man will be wondering where we are."

Mrs. Hunter would fain have kept them, and the last words and compliments were of long duration, while Aurelia looked on in some surprise at the transformation of all Harriet's languishing affected airs into the bustling self-importance of Mrs. Arden. She was however much occupied with all she had heard, and was marvelling how her report would be received in the dark chamber, when her sister began again as soon as they were in the street again. "You are very discreet, Aurelia, as it becomes a young married lady, but have you no notion who this innamorata of the young baronet may be?"

"No, indeed, how should I?"

"I thought he might have confided in your husband, since he makes so sure of his support."

"He has only once come to visit Mr. Belamour, and that was many months ago."

"It is strange," mused Harriet; "Mrs. Dove says she would have taken her Bible oath that it was you, and my Lady believed as much, or she would not have been in such haste to have you wedded. Nay, I'll never believe but he made his confidences to Betty when he came to the Manor House the Sunday after you were gone, though not a word could I get from her."

"It must have been all a mistake," said Aurelia, not without a little twinge at the thought of what might have been. "I wish you would not talk of it."

"Well he could have been but a fickle adorer— 'tis the way of men, my dear, for he must have found some new flame while his mother and the Colonel were both at the Bath. They have proof positive of his riding out of town at sundown, but whither he goes is unknown, for he takes not so much as a groom with him, and he is always in time for morning parade."

"Poor young man, it is hard to be so beset with spies and watchers," said Aurelia.

"Most true," said Harriet, "but I am monstrous glad you are safe married like me, child, so that no one can accuse us. Such romantic affairs are well enough to furnish a course of letters to the *Tatler*, or the *Gentlewomen's Magazine*, but I am thankful for a comfortable life with my good man."

Therewith they reached their inn, where Harriet, having satisfied herself that the said good man was safe within, and profiting by the unwonted calm to write his inaugural sermon, took Aurelia to her bedroom to prepare for dinner, and to indulge in further confidences.

"So, Aurelia, I can report to my father that you are looking well, and as cheerful as can be expected."

"Nay, I have always told you I am happy as the day is long."

"What, when you have never so much as seen your husband?"

"Only at our wedding, and then he was forced to veil his face from the light."

"Nor has he ever seen you?"

"Not unless he then saw me."

"If he were not then charmed enough to repeat the view, you are the most cruelly wasted and unworthily matched—"

"Hush, sister!" broke out Aurelia in eager indignation.

"What! is a lovely young creature, almost equal to what I was before my cruel malady, to waste her bloom on a wretched old melancholic, who will not so much as look at her!"

"Harriet, I cannot hear this—you know not of what you are talking! What is my poor skin-deep beauty—if beauty it be—compared with the stores of goodness and wisdom I find in him?"

"La! child, what heat is this? One would really think you loved him."

"Of course I do! I love and honour him more than any one I ever met—except my dear father."

"Come, Aura, you are talking by rote out of

the marriage service. You may be open with me, you know, it will go no further; and I do long to know whether you can be truly content at heart," said Harriet with real affection.

"Dear sister," said Aurelia, touched, "believe me that indeed I am. Mr. Belamour is kindness itself. He is all he ever promised to be to me, and sometimes more."

"Yet if he loved you, he could never let you live moped up there. Are you never frighted at the dark chamber? I should die of it!"

"The dark does not fright me," said Aurelia.

"You have a courage I have not! Come, now, were you never frighted to talk with a voice in the dark?"

"Scarcely ever!" said Aurelia.

"Scarcely—when was that?"

"You will laugh, Harriet, but it is when he is most—most tender and full of warmth. Then I hardly know him for the same."

"What? If he be not always tender to my poor dear child, he must be a wretch indeed."

"O no, no, Harriet! How shall I ever make

you understand?" cried Aurelia. "Never for a moment is he other than kind and gentle. It is generally like a father, only more courtly and deferential, but sometimes something seems to come over him, and he is—oh! I cannot tell you —what I should think a lover would be," faltered Aurelia, colouring crimson, and hiding her face on her sister's shoulder, as old habits of confidence, and need of counsel and sympathy were obliterating all the warnings of last night.

"You silly little chit! Why don't you encourage these advances? You ought to be charmed, not frightened."

"They would ch——I should like it if it were not so like two men in one, the one holding the other back."

Harriet laughed at this fancy, and Aurelia was impelled to defend it. "Indeed, Harriet, it is really so. There will be whispers—oh, such whispers!"—she sunk her voice and hid her face again—"close to my ear, and—endearments— while the grave voice sounds at the other end of the room, and then I long for light. I swooned for fright the first time, but I am much more used to it now."

"This is serious," said Harriet, with unwonted gravity. "Do you really think that there is another person in the room?"

"I do not feel as if it could be otherwise, and yet it is quite impossible."

"I would not bear it," said her sister. "You ought not to bear it. How do you know that it is not some vile stratagem? It might even be the blackamoor!"

"No, no, Harriet! I know better than that. It is quite impossible. Besides, I am sure of this—that the hands that wedded me are the same hands that caress me," she added, with another blushing effort, "strong but delicate hands, rather hard inside, as with the bridle. I noticed it because once I thought his hands soft with doing nothing and being shut up."

"That convinces me the more, then, there is some strange imposition practised upon you," said Harriet, anxiously.

"Oh, no!" said Aurelia, inconsistently; "Mr.

Belamour is quite incapable of doing anything wrong by me. I cannot let you have such shocking notions. He told me I must be patient and trust him, though I should meet with much that was strange and inexplicable."

"This is trusting him much too far. They are playing on your inexperience, I am sure. If you were not a mere child, you would see what a shocking situation this is."

"I wish I had not told you," said Aurelia, tears rushing into her eyes. "I ought not! He bade me be cautious how I talked, and you have made me quite forget!"

"Did he so? Then it is evident that he fears disclosure! Something must be done. Why not write to our father?"

"I could not! He would call it a silly fancy."

"And it might embroil him with my Lady," added Harriet. "We must devise another mode."

"You will not—must not tell Mr. Arden," exclaimed Aurelia, peremptorily.

"Never fear! He heeds nothing more sublunary than the course of the planets. But I have it. His device will serve the purpose. Do you remember Eugene confounding him with Friar Bacon because he was said to light a candle without flint or steel? It was true. When he was a bachelor he always lit his own candle and fire, and he always carries the means. I was frighted the first time he showed me, but now I can do it as well as he. See," she said, opening a case, "a drop of this spirit upon this prepared cotton;" and as a bright flame sprang up and made Aurelia start, she laughed and applied a taper to it. " There, one such flash would be quite enough to prove to you whether there be any deception practised on you."

"I could never do it! Light is agony to Mr. Belamour, and what would he think?"

"He would take it for lightning, which I suppose he cannot keep out."

"One flash did come through everything last summer, but I was not looking towards him."

"You will be wiser this time. Here, I can give you this little bottle and box, for Mr. Arden compounded a fresh store in town."

"I dare not, sister. He has ever bidden me trust without sight; and you cannot guess how good he is to me, and how noble and generous. I cannot insult him by a doubt."

"Then he should not act as no true woman can endure."

"And it would hurt him."

"Tut, tut, child; if the lightning did not harm him how can this flash? I tell you no man has a right to trifle with you in this manner, and it is your duty to yourself and all of us to find out the truth. Some young rake may have bribed the black, and be personating him; and some day you may find yourself carried off you know not where."

"Harriet, if you only knew either Mr. Belamour or Jumbo, you would know that you are saying things most shocking!"

"Convince me, then! Look here, Aurelia, if you cannot write to me and explain this double-faced or double-voiced husband of yours, I vow to you that I shall speak to Mr. Arden, and write to my father."

"Oh! do not, do not, sister! Remember, it is of

no use unless this temper of affection be on him, and I have not heard it this fortnight, no, nor more."

"Promise me, then, that you will make the experiment. See, here is a little chain-stitch pouch—poor Peggy Duckworth's gift to me—with two pockets. Let me fasten it under your dress, and then you will always have it about you."

"If the bottle broke as I rode home!"

"Impossible; it is a scent-bottle of strong glass."

Here Mr. Arden knocked at the door, regretting to interrupt their confidences, but dinner awaited them; and as, immediately after, Mrs. Hunter brought her husband in his best wig to call on Madame Belamour and her relations, the sisters had no more time together, till the horses were at the door, and they went to their room together to put on their hats.

A whole mass of refusals and declarations of perfect confidence were on Aurelia's tongue, but Harriet cut them all short by saying, "Remember, you are bound for your own honour and ours, to clear up this mystery!"

Then they rode off their several ways, Madame Belamour towards Bowstead, Mr. and Mrs. Arden on their sturdy roadster towards Lea Farm.

CHAPTER III.

A FATAL SPARK.

> And so it chanced: which in those dark
> And fireless halls was quite amazing,
> Did we not know how small a spark
> Can set the torch of love ablazing.
> — T. MOORE.

AURELIA rode home in perplexity, much afraid of the combustibles at her girdle, and hating the task her sister had forced on her. She felt as if her heedless avowals had been high treason to her husband; and yet Harriet was her elder, and those assurances that as a true woman she was bound to clear up the mystery, made her cheeks burn with shame, and her heart thrill with the determination to vindicate her husband, while the longing to know the face of one who so loved her was freshly awakened.

She was strongly inclined to tell him all, indeed she knew herself well enough to be aware that half a dozen searching questions would draw out the whole confession of her own communication and Harriet's unworthy suspicions; and humiliating as this would be, she longed for the opportunity. Here, however, she was checked in her meditations by a stumble of her horse, which proved to have lost a shoe. It was necessary to leave the short cut, and make for the nearest forge, and when the mischief was repaired, to ride home by the high road.

She thus came home much later than had been expected; Jumbo, Molly, and the little girls were all watching for her, and greeted her eagerly. The supper was already on the table for her, and she had only just given Fay and Letty the cakes and comfits she had bought at Brentford for them when Jumbo brought the message that his master hoped that madam, if not too much fatigued, would come to him as soon as her supper was finished.

Accordingly, she came without waiting to

change her dress, having only taken off her hat and arranged her hair.

She felt guilty, and dreaded the being questioned, yet longed to make her avowal and have all explained. The usual greetings passed, and then Mr. Belamour said, "I heard your horse hoofs come in late. You were detained?"

She explained about the shoe, and a few sentences were passing about her sister when she detected a movement, as if a step were stealing towards her, together with a hesitation in the remark Mr. Belamour was making about Mrs. Hunter's good nature.

Quite irrelevantly came in the whispering voice, "Where is my dearest life?"

"Sir, sir!" she cried, driven at last to bay, "what is this? Are you one or two?"

"One with you, my sweetest life! Your own —your husband!"

Therewith there was a kind of groan further off, and as Aurelia felt a hand on her dress, her fright and distress at the duality were complete. While, in the dark, the hands were still groping for her, she eluded them, and succeeded in carrying out Harriet's manœuvre so far that a quick bright flame leapt forth, lighting up the whole room, and revealing two—yes, two! But it did not die away! In her haste, and in the darkness, she had poured the whole contents of the bottle on the phosphoric cotton, and dropped both without knowing it on a chintz curtain. A fresh evening breeze was blowing in from the window, open behind the shutters, and in one second the curtain was a flaming, waving sheet. Some one sprang up to tear it down, leaping on a table in the window. The table overbalanced, the heavy iron curtain-rod came out suddenly, and there was a fall, the flaming mass covering the fallen! The glare shone on a strange white face and head as well as on Jumbo's black one, and with a trampling and crushing the fire died down, quenched as suddenly as it began, and all was obscurity again.

"Nephew, dear boy, speak," exclaimed Mr. Belamour; and as there was no answer, "Open the shutters, Jumbo. For Heaven's sake let us see!"

"Oh! what have I done?" cried poor Aurelia, in horror and misery, dropping by him on the ground, while the opened shutters admitted the twilight of a May evening, with a full moon, disclosing a strange scene. A youth in a livery riding coat lay senseless on the ground, partly covered by the black fragments of the curtain, the iron rod clenched in one hand, the other arm doubled under him. A face absolutely white, with long snowy beard and hair hung over him, and an equally white pair of hands tried to lift the head. Jumbo had in a second sprung down, removed the fallen table, and come to his master's help. "Struck head with this," he said, as he tried to unclasp the fingers from the bar, and pointed to a grazed blow close to the temple.

"We must lay him on my bed," said Mr. Belamour. Then, seeing the girl's horror-stricken countenance, "Ah, child, would that you had been patient; but it was overtasking you! Call Aylward, I beg of you. Tell her he is here, badly hurt. What, you do not know him," as her bewildered eyes and half-opened lips implied the question she could not utter, "you do not know him? Sir Amyas—my nephew—your true husband!"

"Oh! and I have killed him!" she cried, with clasped hands.

"Hush, child, no, with God's mercy! Only call the woman and bring a light."

She rushed away, and appeared, a pale terrified figure, with the smell of fire on her hair and white dress, in the room where Mrs. Aylward was reading her evening chapter. She could scarcely utter her message as she stood under the gaze of blank amazement; but Mrs. Aylward understood enough to make her start up without another word, and hurry away, candle in hand.

Aurelia took up the other, and followed, trembling. When she reached the outer room the rush of air almost blew out her light, and pausing, afraid to pass on, she perceived that Mr. Belamour and Jumbo were carrying the insensible form between them into the inner apartment, while a moan or two filled her heart with pangs of self-reproach.

She hung about, in terrible anxiety, but not daring to come forward while the others were engaged about the sufferer, for what seemed a very long time before she heard Mrs. Aylward say, "His arm is broke, sir. We must send for Dr. Hunter. The maids are all in their beds, but I will go and wake one, and send her to the stables to call the groom."

"I had best go," said Mr. Belamour. "You are of more use than I. He sleeps at the stables, you say?" Then, seeing the waiting, watching form of Aurelia, he said, "Come in, my poor child. Perhaps your voice may rouse him." Every one, including himself, seemed to have forgotten Mr. Belamour's horror of light, for candles were flaring on all the tables, as he led the young girl in, saying, "Speak to him."

At the death-like face in its golden hair, Aurelia's voice choked in her throat, and it was in an unnatural hoarse tone that she tried to say, "Sir— Sir Amyas—"

"I trust he will soon be better," said Mr. Belamour, marking her dismay and grief with his wonted kindness, " but his arm needs the surgeon, and I must be going. Let Lady Belamour sit here, Mrs. Aylward. I trust you with the knowledge. It was my nephew, in disguise, who wedded her, unknown to her. She is entirely blameless. Let Jumbo fetch her a cordial. There, my child, take this chair, so that his eyes may fall on you when he opens them. Bathe his head if you will. I shall return quickly after having sped the groom on his journey."

Gloomy and doubtful were the looks cast on Aurelia by the housekeeper, but all unseen by the wondering, bewildered, remorseful eyes fixed on the white face on the pillow, heedless of its perfect symmetry of feature, and knowing only that this was he who had thrilled her heart with his tender tones, who had loved her so dearly, and dared so much for her sake, but whom her impatience and distrust had so cruelly injured. Had she seen him strong, well, and ardent, as she had so lately heard him, her womanhood would have recoiled indignantly at the deception which had stolen her vows; but the spectacle of the young senseless face and prostrate form filled her with compassion, tenderness, and remorse, for having yielded to her sister's persuasions. With intense anxiety she watched, and assisted in the fomentations, longing for Mr. Belamour's return; but time passed on and still he came not. No words passed, only a few faint sighs, and one of the hands closed tight on Aurelia's.

CHAPTER IV.

WRATH AND DESOLATION.

> Straight down she ran
> .... and fatally did vow
> To wreake her on that mayden messenger
> Whom she had caused be kept as prisonere.
> SPENSER.

HARK! there was the trampling of horses and thundering of wheels at the door! Could the doctor be come already, and in such a fashion?

Jumbo hurried to admit him, and Mrs. Aylward moved to arrange matters, but the clasp that was on Aurelia's hand would not let her go.

Presently there came, not Dr. Hunter's tread, but a crisp, rustling sound, and the tap of high heels, and in the doorway stood, tall, erect, and terrible, Lady Belamour, with a blaze of wrath in her blue eyes, and concentrated rage in her whole form, while in accents low, but coming from between her teeth, she demanded "Miserable boy, what means this?"

"Oh! madam, take care! he is sadly hurt!" cried Aurelia, with a gesture as if to screen him.

"I ask what this means?" repeated Lady Belamour, advancing, and seeming to fill the room with her majestic figure, in full brocaded dress, with feathers waving in her hair.

"His Honour cannot answer you, my Lady," said Mrs. Aylward. "He has had a bad fall, and Mr. Belamour is gone to send for the doctor."

"This is the housekeeping in my absence!" said Lady Belamour, showing less solicitude as to her son's condition than indignation at the discovery, and her eyes and her diamonds glittering fearfully.

"My Lady," said Mrs. Aylward, with stern respectfulness, "I knew nothing of all this till this lady called me an hour ago telling me Sir Amyas was hurt. I found him as you see. Please your Ladyship, I must go back to him."

"Speak then, you little viper," said Lady Belamour, turning on Aurelia, who had risen, but was held fast by the hand upon hers. "By what arts have you well nigh slain my son? Come here, and tell me."

"None, madam!" gasped Aurelia, trembling, so that she grasped her chair-back with her free hand for support. "I never saw him till to-night."

"Lies will not serve you, false girl. Come here this instant! I *know* that you have been shamelessly receiving my son here, night after night."

"I never knew!"

"Missie Madam never knew," chimed in Jumbo. "All in the dark. She thought it old mas'r."

Lady Belamour looked contemptuously incredulous; but the negro's advocacy gave a kind of courage to Aurelia, and availing herself of a slight relaxation of the fingers she withdrew her hand, and coming forward, said, "Indeed, madam, I know nothing, I was entirely deceived. Only hearing two voices in the dark alarmed me, so that I listened to my sister, and struck a light to discover the truth. Then all caught fire, and blazed up, and—"

"Then you are an incendiary as well as a

traitor," said her Ladyship, with cold, triumphant malignity. "This is work for the constable. Here, Loveday," to her own woman, who was waiting in the outer room, "take this person away, and lock her into her own room till morning, when we can give her up to justice."

"Oh, my Lady," cried Aurelia, crouching at her feet and clinging to her dress, "do not be so cruel! Oh! let me go home to my father!"

"Madam!" cried a voice from the bed, "let alone my wife! Come, Aurelia. Oh!"

The starting up in bed had wrenched his broken arm, and he fell back senseless again, just as Aurelia would have flown back to him, but his mother stood between, spurning her away.

Another defender, if she could so be called, spoke for her. "It is true, please your Ladyship," said Mrs. Aylward, "that Mr. Belamour called her the wife of this poor young gentleman."

Jumbo too exclaimed, "No one knew but Jumbo; His Honour marry pretty missie in mas'r's wig and crimson dressing-gown."

"A new stratagem!" ironically observed the

incensed lady. "But your game is played out, miss, for madam I cannot call you. Such a marriage cannot stand for a moment; and if a lawyer like Amyas Belamour pretended it could, either his wits were altogether astray or he grossly deceived you. Or, as I believe, he trafficked with you to entrap this unhappy youth, whose person and house you have, between you, almost destroyed. Remove her, Loveday, and lock her up till we can send for a magistrate to take depositions in the morning. Go quietly, girl, I will not have my son disturbed with your outcries."

Poor Aurelia's voice died in her throat. Oh! why did not Mr. Belamour come to her rescue? Ah! he had bidden her trust and be patient; she had transgressed, and he had abandoned her! There was no sign of life or consciousness in the pallid face on the bed, and with a bleeding heart she let the waiting-maid lead her through the outer apartment, still redolent of the burning, reached her own chamber, heard the key turn in the lock, and fell across her bed in a sort of annihilation.

The threat was unspeakably frightful. Those were days of capital punishment for half the offences in the calendar, and of what was to her scarcely less dreadful, of promiscuous imprisonment, fetters, and gaol fever. Poor Aurelia's ignorance could hardly enhance these horrors, and when her perceptions began to clear themselves, her first thought was of flight from a fate equally dreadful to the guilty or not guilty.

Springing from the bed, she tried the other door of her room, which was level with the wainscoting, and not readily observed by a person unfamiliar with the house. It yielded to her hand, and she knew there was a whole suite of empty rooms thus communicating with one another. It was one of those summer nights that are never absolutely dark, and there was a full moon, so that she had light enough to throw off her conspicuous white habit, all scorched and singed as it was, and to put on her dark blue cloth one, with her camlet cloak and hood. She made up a small bundle of clothes, took her purse, which was well filled with guineas and silver, and moved softly to the door.

Hide and seek had taught her all the modes of eluding observation, and with her walking shoes in her hand, and her feet slippered, she noiselessly crept through one empty room after another, and descended the stair into her own lobby, where she knew how to open the sash door.

One moment the thought that Mr. Belamour would protect her made her pause, but the white phantom she had seen seemed more unreal than the voice she was accustomed to, and both alike had vanished and abandoned her to her fate. Nay, she had been cheated from the first. Everything had given way with her. My Lady might be coming to send her to prison. Hark, some one was coming! She darted out, down the steps, along the path like a wild bird from a cage.

CHAPTER V.

THE WANDERER.

> Widowed wife and wedded maid,
> Betrothed, betrayer, and betrayed.—SCOTT.

AURELIA'S first halt was in a moss-grown summer-house at the end of the garden, where she ventured to sit down to put on her stout leather shoes. The children's toys, a ball and a set of ninepins lay on the floor! How many ages ago was it that she had made that sarcastic reply to Letty?—perhaps her last!

A nightingale, close overhead, burst into a peal of song, repeating his one favourite note, which seemed to her to cry out "Although my heart is broke, broke, broke, broke." The tears rushed into her eyes, but at a noise as of opening doors or windows at the house, terror mastered her again, and she hurried on to hide herself from the dawning light, which was beginning to increase, as she crossed the park, on turf dank with Maydew, and plunged deep into the thick woods beyond, causing many a twittering cry of wondering birds.

Day had fully come, and slanting golden beams were shining through the tender green foliage, and illuminating the boles of the trees, ere she was forced by failing strength again to pause and sit on a faggot, while gathering breath and considering where she should go. Home was her first thought. Who could shield her but her father and sister? How she longed for their comfort and guardianship! But how reach them? She had money but that could do little for her. England never less resembled those days of Brian Boromhe when the maiden with the gems rich and rare wandered unscathed from sea to sea in Ireland. Post chaises, though coming into use, had not dawned on the simple country girl's imagination. She knew there was a weekly coach from London to Bath, passing through Brentford, and that place was also a great starting-place for stage waggons, of which one went through Carminster, but her bewildered brain could not recall on what day it started, and there was an additional shock of despair when she remembered that it was Sunday morning. The chill of the morning dew was on her limbs, she was exhausted by her fatigues of the night, a drowsy recollection of the children in the wood came over her, and she sank into a dreamy state that soon became actual sleep. She was wakened by a strong bright sunbeam on her eyes, and found that this was what had warmed her limbs in her sleep. A sound as of singing was also in her ears, and of calling cows to be milked. She did not in the least know where she was, for she had wandered into parts of the wood quite strange to her, but she thought she must be a great way from home, and quite beyond recognition, so she followed the voice, and soon came out on a tiny meadow glade, where a stout girl was milking a great sheeted cow.

She knew now that she was faint with hunger and thirst, and must take food before she could go much farther, so taking out a groat, her smallest coin, she accosted the girl, and offered it for a draught of milk. To her dismay the girl exclaimed "Lawk! It be young Madam! Sarvice, ma'am!"

"I have lost myself in the wood," said Aurelia. "I should be much obliged for a little milk."

"Well to be sure. Think of that! And have ee been out all night? Ye looks whisht!" said the girl, readily filling a wooden cup she had brought with her, for in those days good new milk was a luxury far more easily accessible than in ours. She added a piece of barley bread, her own intended breakfast, and was full of respectful wonder, pity, and curiosity, proposing that young Madam should come and rest in mother's cottage in the wood, and offering to guide her home as soon as the cows were milked and the pigs fed. Aurelia had some difficulty in shaking her off, finding also that she had gone round and round in the labyrinthine paths, and was much nearer the village of Bowstead than she had intended.

Indeed, she was obliged to deceive the kindly girl by walking off in the direction she pointed out, intending to strike afterwards into another path, though where to go she had little idea, so long as it was out of reach of my Lady and her prison.

Oh! if Harriet were only at Brentford, or if it were possible to reach the Lea Farm where she was! Could she ask her way thither, or could she find some shelter near or in Brentford till the coach or the waggon started? This was the most definite idea her brain, refreshed somewhat by the food, could form; but in the meantime she was again getting bewildered in the field paths. It was a part she did not know, lying between the backs of the cottages and their gardens, and the woods belonging to the great house; and the long sloping meadows, spangled with cowslips were much alike. The cowslips seemed to strike her with a pang as she recollected her merry day among them last spring, and how little she then thought of being a homeless wanderer. At last, scarce knowing where she was, she sat down on the step of a stile leading to a little farmyard, leant her head on the top bar and wept bitterly.

Again she was startled by hearing a voice

saying, "Sister, what is that in the field?" and, starting up, she saw Mrs. Delia in high pattens, and her Sunday silk tucked up over her quilted petticoat, with a basket of corn in her hand, surrounded by her poultry, while Mrs. Phœbe was bending over a coop. She had stumbled unawares on their back premises, and with a wild hope, founded on their well-known enmity to Lady Belamour, she sprang over the stile. Mrs. Delia retreated in haste, but Mrs. Phœbe came to the front.

"Oh! Mrs. Phœbe," she cried, "I ask your pardon."

"Mrs. Belamour! Upon my word! To what are we indebted for this visit?"

"Oh! of your kindness listen to me, madam," said Aurelia. "My Lady is come, and there is some dreadful mistake, and she is very angry with me; and if you would only take me in and hide me till the waggon goes and I can get home!"

"So my Lady has found you out, you artful hussy," returned Mrs. Phœbe. "I have long guessed at your tricks! I knew it was no blackamoor that was stealing into the great house."

"I do not know what you mean."

"Oh! it is of no use to try your feigned artlessness on us. I wonder at your assurance, after playing false with uncle and nephew both at once."

"If you would but hear me!"

"I have heard enough of you already. I wonder you dare show your face at a respectable house. Away with you, if you would not have me send the constable after you!"

The threat renewed Aurelia's terror, and again she fled, but this time she fell into a path better known to her, that leading to Sedhurst, and ultimately to Brentford.

The recollection of Dame Wheatfield's genial good nature inspired her with another hope, and she made her way towards the farm. The church bells were ringing, and she saw the farmer and his children going towards the church, but not the mistress, and she might therefore hope to find her at home and alone. As she approached, a great dog began a formidable barking, and his voice brought out the good woman in person. " Down, Bouncer! A won't hurt'ee, my lass. What d'ye lack that you bain't at church?"

"May I speak to you, Mrs. Wheatfield?"

"My stars, if it bain't young Miss—Madam, I mean! Nothing ain't wrong with the child?"

"O no, she is quite well, but—"

"What, ye be late for church? Come in and sit ye down a bit, and take a bit and sup after your walk. We have been and killed Spotty's calf, though 'twas but a staggering Bob, but us couldn't spare the milk no longer. So we've got the l'in on un for dinner, and you're kindly welcome if you ain't too proud. Only I wish you had brought my little missie."

"O Mrs. Wheatfield! Shall I ever see the dear little girl again? Oh! can you help me? Do you know where Lea Farm is? I'd pay anything for a horse and man to take me there, where my sister is staying."

"Well, I don't know as my master would hire a horse out of a Sunday, unless 'twere very particler—illness or suchlike. Lea Farm did you say ma'am? Is it the Lea out by Windmill hill—Master Brown's; or Lea Farm, down by the river—Tom Smith's?"

"No, this is Mr. Meadows's, a grazier."

"Never heard tell on him, ma'am, but the master might, when he comes in. But bless me," she added, after a moment's consideration, "what will the master say? He'll be asking how it comes that a lady like you, with a coach and horses of her own, should be coming after a horse here. You ain't been and got into trouble with my Lady, my dear?"

"Oh! Dame, indeed I have; pray help me!"

It was no wonder that Mrs. Wheatfield failed to gather more than that young Madam had almost burnt the house, and had fallen under grievous displeasure, so as even to fear the constable.

"Bless your poor heart! Think of that now! But I'm afeard we can't do nothing for you. My master would be nigh about killing me if I harboured you and got him into trouble, with the gentry."

"If you could only hide me in some loft or barn till I could meet the coach for Bath! Then I should be almost at home."

"I dare not. The children are routing about everywhere on a Sunday afternoon; and if so be as there's a warrant out after you" (Aurelia shuddered) "my man would be mad with me. He ain't never forgot how his grandfather was hanged up there in that very walnut for changing clothes with a young gentleman in the wars long ago."

"Then I must go! Oh, what will become of me?"

"Stay a bit! It goes to my heart to turn you from the door, and you so white and faint. And they won't be out of church yet a while. You've ate nothing all this time! What was you thinking of doing, my dear?"

"I don't know. If I could only find out the right Lea Farm, and get a man and horse to take me there—but my sister goes on Monday, and I might not find her, and nobody knows where it is. And nobody will take me in or hide me till the coach goes! Oh, what will become of me?"

"It is bitter hard," said the Dame. "I wish to my heart I could take you in, but you see there's the master! I'll tell you what: there's my cousin, Patty Woodman; she might take you in for a night or two. But you'd never find your way to her cot; it lies out beyond the spinneys. I must show you the way. Look you here. Nobody can't touch you in a church, they hain't got no power there, and if you would slip into that there empty place as opens with the little door, as the ringers goes in by, afore morning prayers is over I'll make an excuse to come to evening prayer alone, or only with little Davy, as is lying asleep there. If Patty is there I'll speak, and you can go home with her. If not, I must e'en walk with you out to the spinney. Hern is a poor place, but her's a good sort of body, and won't let you come to no harm; and her goes into Brentford with berries and strawberries to meet the coaches, so may be she'll know the day."

"Oh, thank you, thank you, dear Mrs. Wheatfield! If I can only get safe home!"

"Come, don't be in haste. You'll take a bit of bread and cheese, and just a draught of ale to hearten you up a bit."

Aurelia was too sick at heart for food, and feared to delay, lest she should meet the congregation, but Mrs. Wheatfield forced on her a little basket with some provisions, and she gladly accepted another draught of milk.

No one came out by the little door she was told; all she had to do would be to keep out of sight when the ringers came in before the afternoon service. She knew the way, and was soon close to Mary Sedhurst's grave. "Ah! why was he not constant to her," she thought; "and oh! why has he deserted me in my need?"

The little door easily yielded, and she found herself—after passing the staircase-turret that led by a gallery to the belfry in the centre of the church—in an exceedingly dilapidated transept;

once, no doubt, it had been beautiful, before the coloured glass of the floriated window had been knocked out and its place supplied with bricks. The broken effigy of a crusading Sedhurst, devoid of arms, feet, and nose was stowed away in the eastern sepulchre, in company with funeral apparatus, torn books, and moth-eaten cushions; but this would not have shocked her even in calmer moments. She only cared to find a corner where she was entirely sheltered, between a green stained pier and the high wall and curtain of a gigantic pew, where no doubt sweet Mary Sedhurst had once worshipped. The lusty voices of the village choir in some exalted gallery beyond her view were shouting out a familiar tune, and with some of Betty's mild superstition about "the singing psalms," she heard—

> "Since I have placed my trust in God,
> A refuge always nigh,
> Why should I, like a tim'rous bird
> To distant mountains fly?
>
> "Behold the wicked bend their bow,
> And ready fix their dart,
> Lurking in ambush to destroy
> The man of upright heart.

> "When once the firm assurance fails
> Which public faith imparts,
> 'Tis time for innocence to flee
> From such deceitful arts.
>
> "The Lord hath both a temple here
> And righteous throne above,
> Whence He surveys the sons of men,
> And how their counsels move."

Poor timorous bird, whom even the firm assurance of wedded faith had failed, what was left to her but to flee from the darts levelled against her? Yet that last verse brought a sense of protection. Ah! did she deserve it? A prayerless night and prayerless morning had been hers, and no wonder, since she had never gone to bed nor risen with the ordinary forms; but it was with a pang that she recollected that the habit of calling out in her heart for guidance and help had been slipping from her for a long time past, and she had never asked for heavenly aid when her judgment was perplexed by Harriet, no, nor for protection in her flight.

She resolved to say her morning prayers with full attention so soon as the church was empty, and meantime to follow the service with all her powers, though her pulses were still throbbing and her head aching.

In the far distance she heard the Commandments, and near to her the unseen clerk responding, and then followed a gospel of love and comfort. She could not catch every word, but there was a sense of promised peace and comfort, which began to soothe the fluttering heart, for the first time enjoying a respite from the immediate gripe of deadly terror.

The sermon chimed in with these feelings, not that she could have given any account of it, nor preserved any connected memory, but it was full of the words, Faith, Love, Sacrifice, so that they were borne in on her ear and thought. Heavenly Love surrounding as with an atmosphere those who had only faith to "taste and see how gracious the Lord is," believing that which cannot be seen, and therefore having it revealed to their inmost senses, and thus living the only real life.

This was the chief thought that penetrated to her mind as she crouched on the straw hassock behind the pew, and shared unseen in the blessing of peace. No one saw her as the hob-nailed shoes trooped out of church, and soon she was entirely alone, kneeling still in her hiding-place, and whispering half-aloud the omitted morning prayer, whose heartfelt signification had, she felt, been neglected for a long, long time.

Since when? Ah! ever since those strange mysterious voices and caresses had come to charm and terrify her, and when her very perplexity should have warned her to cling closer to the aid of her Heavenly Father. Vague yearnings, uplifted feelings, discontents, and little tempers had usurped the place of higher feelings, and blinded her eyes. And through it all, her heart began to ache and long for tidings of him on whose pale features she had gazed so long and who had ventured and suffered so much for her, nay, who had started into a moment's life for her protection! All the tumult of resentment at the deception practised on her fell on the uncle rather than the nephew; and in spite of this long year of tender kindness and consideration from the recluse, there was a certain leaping of heart at finding herself bound not to him but to the youth whose endearments returned with a flood of tender remembrance. And she had fled just as he had claimed her as his wife, unheeding whether he died of the injury she had caused him! All that justified her alarm was forgotten, her heartstrings had wound themselves round him, and began to pull her back.

Then she thought of the danger of directing Lady Belamour's wrath on her father, and leading to his expulsion and destitution. She had been sent from home, and bestowed in marriage to prevent his ruin, and should she now ensure it? Her return to him or even her disappearance would no doubt lead to high words from him, and then he would be cast out to beggary in his old age. No, she could only save him by yielding herself up, exonerating him from all knowledge of her strange marriage, far more of the catastrophe, and let my Lady do her worst! She had, as she knew, not been going on well lately, but she had confessed her faults, and recovered her confidence that her Heavenly Father would guard her as long as she resolutely did her duty. And her duty, as daughter and a wife, if indeed she was one, was surely to return, where her heart was drawing her. It might be very terrible, but still it was going nearer to *him*, and it would save her father.

The door was still open; she wrote a few words of gratitude and explanation to Dame Wheatfield, on a piece of a torn book, wrapped a couple of guineas in it, and laid it in the basket, then, kneeling again to implore protection and safety, and if it might be, forgiveness and reconciliation, she set forth. "Love is strong as death," said Mary Sedhurst's tomb. She knew better what that meant than when her childish eyes first fell upon it. A sense of Divine Love was wrapping her round with a feeling of support and trust, while the human love drew her onwards to confront all deadly possibilities in the hope of rejoining her husband, or at least of averting misfortune from her father.

CHAPTER VI.

VANISHED.

> Where there is no place
>   For the glow-worm to lie,
> Where there is no space
>   For receipt of a fly,
> Where the midge dares not venture
>   Lest herself fast she lay,
> If Love come, he will enter
>   And find out the way.—OLD SONG.

MAJOR DELAVIE and his eldest daughter were sitting down to supper in the twilight, when a trampling of horses was heard in the lane, a carriage was seen at the gate, and up the pathway came a slender youthful figure, in a scarlet coat, with an arm in a sling.

"It is!—yes, it is!" exclaimed Betty: "Sir Amyas himself!"

"Folly, child! Yet—by all the powers, it is! And hurt too!"

In spite of his lameness, the Major had opened the door before Palmer could reach it; but his greeting and inquiry were cut short by the young man's breathless question: "Is she here?"

"Who?"

"My wife—my love. Your daughter, sweet Aurelia! Ah! it was my one hope."

"Come in, come in, sir," entreated Betty, seeing how fearfully pale he grew. "What has befallen you, and where is my sister?"

"Would that I knew! I trusted to have found her here; but now, sir, you will come with me and find her!"

"I do not understand you, sir," said the Major severely, "nor how you are concerned in the matter. My daughter is the wife of your uncle, Mr. Belamour, and if, as I fear, you bear the marks of a duel in consequence of any levity towards her, I shall not find it easy to forgive."

"On my word and honour it is no such thing," said the youth, raising a face full of frank innocence: "Your daughter is my wife, my most dear and precious wife, with full consent and knowledge of my uncle. I was married to her in his clothes, in the darkened room, our names being the same!"

"Was this your promise?" Betty exclaimed.

"Miss Delavie, to the best of my ability I have kept my promise. Your sister has never seen me, nor to her knowledge spoken with me."

"These are riddles, young man," said the Major sternly. "If all be not well with my innocent child, I shall know how to demand an account."

"Sir," said the youth: "I swear to you that she is the same innocent maiden as when she left you. Oh!" he added with a gesture of earnest entreaty, "blame me as you will, only trace her."

"Sit down, and let us hear," said Betty kindly, pushing a chair towards him and pouring out a glass of wine. He sank into the first, but waved aside the second, becoming however so pale that the Major sprang to hold the wine to his lips saying: "Drink, boy, I say!"

"Not unless you forgive me," he replied in a hoarse, exhausted voice.

"Forgive! Of course, I forgive, if you have done no wrong by my child. I see, I see, 'tis not wilfully. You have been hurt in her defence."

"Not exactly," he said: "I have much to tell," but the words came slowly, and there was a dazed weariness about his eye that made Betty say, in spite of her anxiety—"You cannot till you have eaten, and rested. If only one word to say where she is!"

"Oh! that I could! My hope was to find her here," and he was choked by a great strangling sob, which his youthful manhood sought to restrain.

Betty perceived that he was far from being recovered from the injury he had suffered, and did her best to restrain her own and her father's anxiety till she had persuaded him to swallow some of the excellent coffee which Nannerl always made at sight of a guest. To her father's questions meantime, he had answered that he had broken his arm ten days ago, but he could not wait, he had posted down as soon as he could move.

"You ought to sleep before you tell us farther," said the Major, speaking from a strong sense of the duties of a host; but he was relieved when the youth answered, "You are very good, sir, but I could not sleep till you know all."

"Speak, then," said the Major, "I cannot look at your honest young countenance and think you guilty of more than disobedient folly; but I fear it may have cost my poor child very dear! Is it your mother that you dread?"

"I would be thankful even to know her in my mother's keeping!" he said.

"Is there no mistake?" said the Major; "my daughter, Mrs. Arden, saw her at Brentford, safe and blooming."

"Oh, that was before—before—" said Sir Amyas, "the day before she fled from my mother at Bowstead, and has been seen no more."

He put his hand over his face, and bowed it on the table in such overpowering grief as checked the exclamations of horror and dismay and the wrathful demands that were rising to the lips of his auditors, and they only looked at one another in speechless sorrow. Presently he recovered enough to say, "Have patience with me, and I will try to explain all. My cousin, Miss Delavie, knows that I loved her sweet sister from the moment I saw her, and that I hurried to London in the hope of meeting her at my mother's house. On the contrary, my mother, finding it vain to deny all knowledge of her, led me to believe that she was boarded at a young ladies' school with my little sisters. I lived on the vain hope of the holidays, and meantime every effort was made to drive me into a marriage which my very soul abhorred, the contract being absolutely made by the two ladies, the mothers, without my participation, nay, against my protest. I was to be cajoled or else persecuted into it—sold, in fact, that my mother's debts might be paid before her husband's return! I knew my Uncle Belamour was my sole true personal guardian, though he had never acted further than by affixing his signature when needed. I ought to have gone long before to see him, but as I now understand, obstacles had been purposely placed in my way, while my neglectful reluctance was encouraged. It was in the forlorn hope of finding in him a resource that took me to Bowstead at last, and then it was that I learnt how far my mother could carry deception. There I found my sisters, and learnt that my own sweetest life had been placed there likewise. She was that afternoon visiting some old ladies, but my uncle represented that my meeting her could only cause her trouble and lead to her being removed. I was forced then to yield, having an engagement in London that it would have been fatal to break, but I came again at dark, and having sworn me to silence, he was forced to let me take advantage of the darkness of his chamber to listen to her enchanting voice. He promised to help me, as far as he had the power, in resisting the hateful Aresfield engagement, and he obtained the assistance of an old friend in making himself acquainted with the terms of his guardianship, and likewise of a letter my father had left for him. He has given me leave to show a part of it to you, sir," he added, "you will see that my father expressed a strong opinion that you were wronged in the matter of the estates, and declared that he had hoped to make some compensation by a contract between one of your daughters and my brother who died. He charged my uncle if possible to endeavour to bring about such a match between one of your children and myself. Thus, you see, I was acting in the strictest obedience. You shall see the letter at once, if I may bid my fellow Gray bring my pocket-book from my valise."

"I doubt not of your words, my young friend; your father was a gentleman of a high and scrupulous honour. But why all this hide-and-seek work?—I hate holes and corners!"

"You will see how we were driven, sir. My mother came in her turn to see my uncle, and obtain his sanction to her cherished plan, and when he absolutely refused, on account of Lady Aresfield's notorious character, if for no other, she made him understand that nothing would be easier than to get him declared a lunatic and thus to dispense with his consent. Then, finding how the sweet society of your dear daughter had restored him to new life and spirit, she devised the notable expedient of removing what she suspected to be the chief cause of my contumacy, by marrying the poor child to him. He scouted the idea as a preposterous and cruel sacrifice, but it presently appeared that Colonel Mar was ready to find her a debauched old lieutenant who would gladly marry—what do I say?—it profanes the word—but accept the young lady for a couple of hundred pounds. Then did I implore my uncle to seem to yield, and permit me to personate him at the ceremony. Our names being the same, and all being done in private and in the dark, the whole was quite possible, and it seemed the only means of saving her from a terrible fate."

"He might—or you might, have remembered that she had a father!" said the Major.

"True, but you were at a distance, and my mother's displeasure against you was to be deprecated."

"I had rather she had been offended fifty times

than have had such practices with my poor little girl!" said Major Delavie. "No wonder the proposals struck me as strange and ambiguous. Whose writing was it?"

"Mine, at his dictation," said the youth. "He was unwilling, but my importunity was backed by my mother's threats, conveyed through Hargrave, that unless Aurelia became his wife she should be disposed of otherwise, and that his sanity might be inquired into. Hargrave, who is much attached to my uncle, and is in great awe of my Lady, was thoroughly frightened, and implored him to secure himself and the young lady by consenting, thinking, too, that anything that would rouse him would be beneficial."

"It is strange!" mused the Major. "A clear-headed, punctilious man like your uncle, to lend himself to a false marriage! His ten years of melancholy must have changed him greatly!"

"Less than you suppose, sir; but you will remember that my mother is esteemed as a terrible power by all concerned with her. Even when she seemed to love me tenderly, I was made to know what it was to cross her will, and alas! she always carries her point."

"It did seem a mode of protection," said Betty, more kindly.

"And," added the youth, "my uncle impressed on me from the first that he only consented on condition that I treated this wedlock as betrothal alone, never met my sweet love save in his dark room, and never revealed myself to her. He said it was a mere expedient for guarding her until I shall come of age, or Mr. Wayland comes home, when I shall woo her openly, and if needful, repeat the ceremony with her full knowledge. Meanwhile I wrote the whole to my stepfather, and am amazed that he has never written nor come home."

"That is the only rational thing I have heard," said the Major. "Though—did your uncle expect your young blood to keep the terms?"

"Indeed, sir, I was frightened enough the first evening that I ventured on any advances, for they startled her enough to make her swoon away. I carried her from her room, and my uncle dragged me back before the colour came back to that lovely face, so that the women might come to her. That was the only time I ever saw her save through the chinks of the shutters. Judge of the distraction I lived in!"

Betty looked shocked, but her father chuckled a little, though he maintained his tone of censure. " And may I inquire how often these distracting interviews took place?"

" Cruelly seldom for one to whom they were life itself! Mar is, as you know, colonel of my corps, and my liberty has been restrained as much as possible; I believe I have been oftener on guard and on court-martial than any officer of my standing in the service; but about once in a fortnight I could contrive to ride down to a little wayside inn where I kept a fresh horse, also a livery coat and hat. I tied up my horse in a barn on the borders of the park, and put on a black vizard, so as to pass for my uncle's negro in the dark. I could get admittance to my uncle's rooms unknown to any servant save the faithful Jumbo—who has been the sole depository of our secret. However, since my mother's return from Bath, where the compact with Lady Aresfield was fully determined, the persecution has been fiercer. I may have aroused suspicion by failing to act my part when she triumphantly announced my uncle's marriage to me, or else by my unabated resistance to the little termagant who is to be forced on me. At any rate, I have been so intolerably watched whenever I was not on duty, that my hours of bliss became rarer than ever. Well, sir, my uncle charges me with indiscretion, and says my ardour aroused unreasonable suspicions. He was constantly anxious, and would baulk me in my happiest and most tantalising moments by making some excuse for breaking up the evening, and then would drive me frantic by asking whether he was to keep up my character for consistency in my absence. However, ten days since, the twelfth of May, after three weeks' unendurable detention in town on one pretext or another, I escaped, and made my way to Bowstead at last. My uncle told me that he had been obliged unwillingly to consent to our precious charge going to meet her sister at Brentford, and that she was but newly come home. Presently she entered, but scarcely had I accosted her before a blaze broke out close to us. The flame caught the dry old curtains, they flamed up like tinder, and as I leaped up on a table to tear them down, it gave way with me, I got a blow on the head, and knew no more. It seems that my uncle, as soon as the fire was out, finding that my arm was broken, set out to send the groom for the doctor—he being used to range the park at night. The stupid fellow, coming home half tipsy from the village, saw his white hair and beard in the moonlight, took him for a ghost, and ran off headlong. Thereupon my uncle, with new energy in the time of need, saddled the horse, changed his dressing-gown for the groom's coat, and rode off to Brentford. Then, finding that Dr. Hunter was not within, he actually went on to London, where Dr. Sandys, who had attended him ever since his wound, forced him to go to bed, and to remain there till his own return. Thus my darling had no one to protect her, when, an hour or so after the accident, my mother suddenly appeared. Spies had been set on me by Mar, and so soon as they had brought intelligence of my movements she had hurried off from Ranelagh, in full dress, just as she was, to track and surprise me. My uncle, having gone by the bridle path, had not met her, and I was only beginning to return to my senses. I have a dim recollection of hearing my mother threatening and accusing Aurelia, and striving to interfere, but I was as one bound down, and all after that is blank to me. When my understanding again became clear, I could only learn that my mother had locked her into her own room, whence she had escaped, and"—with a groan—"nothing has been heard of her since!" Again he dropped his head on his hand as one in utter dejection.

"Fled! What has been done to trace her?" cried the Major.

"Nothing could be done till my mother was gone and my uncle returned. The delirium was on me, and whatever I tried to say turned to raving, all the worse if I saw or heard my mother, till Dr. Sandys forbade her coming near me. She was invited to the Queen's Sunday card party moreover, so she fortunately quitted Bowstead just before Mr. Belamour's return."

"Poor gentleman, he could do nothing," said Betty.

"Indeed I should have thought so, but it seems that he only needed a shock to rouse him. His state had become hypochondriacal, and this strong emotion has caused him to exert himself; and when he came into the daylight, he found he could bear it. I could scarce believe my eyes when, on awakening from a sleep, I found him by my bedside, promising me that if I would only remain still, he would use every endeavour to recover the dear one. He went first to Brentford, thinking she might have joined her sister there, but Mr. and Mrs. Arden had left it at the same time as she did. Then he travelled on to their Rectory at Rundell Canonicorum, thinking she might have followed them, but they had only just arrived, and had heard nothing of her; and he next sought her with his friend the Canon of Windsor, but all in vain. Meantime my mother had visited me, and denied all knowledge of her, only carrying away my little sisters, I believe because she found them on either side of my bed, telling me tales of their dear Cousin Aura's kindness. When my uncle returned to Bowstead I could bear inaction no longer, and profited by my sick leave to travel down hither, trusting that she might have found her way to her home, and longing to confess all and implore your pardon, sir—and, alas! your aid in seeking her."

With the large tears in his eyes, the youth rose from his chair as he spoke, and knelt on one knee before the Major, who exclaimed, extremely affected—"By all that is sacred, you have it, my dear boy. It is a wretched affair, but you meant to act honourably throughout, and you have suffered heavily. May God bless you both, and give us back my dear child. My Lady must have been very hard with her, to make her thus fly, all alone."

"You do not know, I suppose, any cause for so timid a creature preferring flight to a little restraint?"

"It seems," said Sir Amyas sadly, "that something the dear girl said gave colour to the charge of having caused the fire, and that my mother in her first passion threatened her with the constable!"

"My poor Aurelia! that might well scare her," cried Betty: "but how could it be?"

"They say she spoke of using something her sister had given her to discover what the mystery was that alarmed her."

"Ah! that gunpowder trick of Mr. Arden's—I always hated it!" exclaimed Betty.

"Gunpowder indeed!" growled the old soldier. "Well, if ever there's mischief among the children, Harriet is always at the bottom of it. I hope Mr. Belamour made her confess if she had a hand in it."

"I believe he did," said Sir Amyas.

"Just like her to set the match to the train and then run away," said the Major.

"Still, sir," said Betty, her womanhood roused to defence, "though I am angered and grieved enough that Harriet should have left Aurelia to face the consequences of the act she instigated,

I must confess that even by Sir Amyas's own showing, if he will allow me to say so, my sisters were justified in wishing to understand the truth."

"That is what my uncle tells me," said the baronet. "He declares that if I had attended to his stipulations, restrained my fervour, or kept my distance, there would have been neither suspicion nor alarm. As if I had not restrained myself!"

"Ay, I dare say," said the Major, a little amused.

"Well, sir, what could a man do with the most bewitching creature in the world, his own wife, too, on the next chair to him?"

There was a simplicity about the stripling—for he was hardly more—which forced them to forgive him; besides, they were touched by his paleness and fatigue. His own man—a respectable elderly servant whom the Major recollected waiting on Sir Jovian—came to beg that his honour would sit up no longer, as he had been travelling since six in the morning, and was quite worn out. Indeed, so it proved; for when the Major and Betty not only promised to come with him on the search the next day, but bade him a kind affectionate good-night. the poor lad, all unused to kindness, fairly burst into tears, which all his dawning manhood could not restrain.

CHAPTER VII.

THE TRACES.

Oh, if I were an eagle to soar into the sky,
I'd gaze around with piercing eye when I my love might spy.

THE second-best coach, which resided at Bowstead, the same which had carried Aurelia off from Knightsbridge, had brought Sir Amyas Belamour to Carminster—an effeminate proceeding of which he was rather ashamed, though clearly he could not have ridden, and he had hoped to have brought his bride back in it.

There was plenty of room in it to take back the Major, Betty, and even Eugene, since he could not well have been left without his sister or Palmer, who was indispensable to the Major. He was so enchanted at "riding in a coach," and going perhaps to see London, that he did not trouble himself much about sister Aurelia being lost, and was in such high spirits as to be best disposed of outside, between Palmer and Gray, where he could at his ease contemplate the horses, generally four in number, though at some stages only two could be procured, and then at an extra steep hill a farmer's horses from the hayfield would be hitched on in front. Luckily there was no lack of money; Mr. Belamour and Hargrave had taken care that Sir Amyas should be amply supplied, and thus the journey was as rapid as posting could be in those days of insufficient inns, worse roads, and necessary precautions against highwaymen.

The road was not the same as that which the young baronet had come down by, as it was thought better to take the chance of meeting a different stage waggon, Sir Amyas and his servant having, of course, examined the one they had overtaken in coming down. At every possible resting place on the route was inquiry made, but all in vain; no one had seen such a young gentlewoman as was described, or if some answer inspired hope for a moment, it was dashed again at once. The young gentlewoman once turned out to be the Squire's fat lady, and another time was actually pursued into a troop of strolling players, attiring themselves in a barn, whence she came with cheeks freshly rouged with blood taken from a cat's tail.

The young baronet had meanwhile become very dear to the Major and his daughter. He had inherited his mother's indescribable attractiveness, and he was so frank, so affectionate, so unspoilt, so grateful for the little attentions demanded by his maimed condition, so considerate of the Major, and so regardless of himself, and, above all, so passionately devoted to his dearest life, as he called Aurelia, that it was impossible not to take him into their hearts, and let him be, as he entreated, a son and a brother.

The travellers decided on first repairing to Bowstead, thinking it probable that the truant might have returned thither, or that Mr. Belamour might have found her in some one of the cottages around. Hopes began to rise, and Major Delavie scolded Sir Amyas in quite a paternal manner whenever he began to despond, though the parts were reversed whenever the young people's expectations began to soar beyond his own spirits at the moment.

"Is yonder Hargrave? No, it is almost like my father!" exclaimed Sir Amyas, in amazement, as the coach lumbered slowly up the approach, and a very remarkable figure was before them. The long white beard was gone, the hair was brushed back, tied up, and the ends disposed of in a square black silk bag, hanging down behind; and the dark grey coat, with collar and deep cuffs of black velvet, was such as would be the ordinary wear of an elderly man of good position; but the face, a fine aquiline one, as to feature, was of perfectly absolute whiteness, scarcely relieved by the thin pale lips, or the eyes, which, naturally of a light-grey, had become almost as colourless as the rest of the face, and Betty felt a shock as if she had seen a marble statue clothed and animated, bowing and speaking.

The anxious inquiry and the mournful negative

had been mutually exchanged before the carriage door was opened, and all were standing together in the avenue.

"I have, however, found a clue, or what may so prove," said Mr. Belamour, when the greetings had passed. "I have discovered how our fugitive passed the early part of the Sunday;" and he related how he had elicited from the Mistresses Treforth that they had seen her and driven her away with contumely.

Sir Amyas and the Major were not sparing of interjections, and the former hoped that his uncle had told them what they deserved.

"Thereby only incurring the more compassion," said Mr. Belamour, drily, and going on to say that he had extended his inquiries to Sedhurst, and had heard of her visit to Dame Wheatfield; also, that the good woman, going to seek her at the church, had found only the basket with the guineas in the paper. She had regarded this merely as a wrapper, and, being unable to read, had never noticed the writing, but she had fortunately preserved it, and Mr. Belamour thus learnt Aurelia's intention of throwing herself on Lady Belamour's mercy.

"My mother utterly denied all knowledge of her, when I cried out to her in anguish when she came to see me!" said Sir Amyas.

"So she does to Hargrave, whom she sent off to interrogate Mrs. Arden," said Mr. Belamour.

"Have you any reason to think the child could have reached my Lady?" inquired Betty, seeing that none of the gentlemen regarded my Lady's denials as making any difference to their belief, though not one of them chose to say so.

"Merely negative evidence," said Mr. Belamour. "I find that no one in the house actually beheld the departure of my Lady on that Sunday afternoon. The little girls had been found troublesome, and sent out into the park with Molly, and my nephew was giving full employment to Jumbo and Mrs. Aylward in my room. The groom, who was at the horses' heads, once averred that he saw two women get into the carriage besides her ladyship; but he is such a sodden, confused fellow, and so contradicts himself, that I can make nothing of him."

"He would surely know his young mistress," said Sir Amyas.

"Perhaps not in the camlet hood, which Dame Wheatfield says she wore."

"Was good old Dove acting as coachman?" said Betty. "We should learn something from him."

"It was not her own coach," said Mr. Belamour. "All the servants were strangers, the liveries sanguine, and the panels painted with helmets and trophies."

"Mar's," said Sir Amyas, low and bitterly.

"I guessed as much," said his uncle. "It was propably chosen on purpose, if the child has friends in your own household."

"Then I must demand her," said the Major. "She cannot be denied to her father."

"At any rate we must go to town to-morrow," said Mr. Belamour. "We have done all we can here."

"Let us send for horses and go on at once," cried Sir Amyas.

"Not so fast, nephew. I see, by her face, that Miss Delavie does not approve, though our side of the town is safer than Hounslow."

"I was not thinking of highwaymen, sir, but we set forth at five this morning, and Sir Amyas always becomes flushed and feverish if he is over fatigued; nor is my father so strong as he was."

"Ah, ha! young sir, in adopting Betty for a sister you find you have adopted a quartermaster-general, eh?" said the Major; "but she is quite right. We should not get to town before ten or eleven at night, and what good would that do? No, no, let us sup and have a good night's rest, and we will drive into town long enough before fine ladies are astir in the morning, whatever may be the fashionable hour nowadays."

"Yes, nephew, you must content yourself with acting host to your father and sister-in-law in your own house," said his uncle.

"It seems to me more like yours, sir," rejoined the youth; but at the hall door, with all his native grace, he turned and gave his welcome, kissing Betty on the cheek with the grave ceremony of the host, and lamenting, poor fellow, that he stood alone without his sweet bride to receive them.

"Is that Jumbo?" asked Betty. "I must thank him for all his kind service to my dear sister."

Faithful Jumbo fairly wept when—infinite condescension for those days—Major Delavie shook hands with him and thanked him.

"If pretty Missie Madam were but safe and well, Jumbo would wish no more," he sobbed out.

"Poor Jumbo," said Mr. Belamour, "he has never been the same man since pretty Missie Madam has been lost. I hear his violin mourning for her till it is enough to break one's heart!"

However Eugene created a diversion by curious inquiries whether Jumbo would indeed play the fiddle of which he had heard from Archer and Amoret, and he ran off most eagerly after the negro to be introduced to the various curiosities of the place.

Mrs. Aylward attended Miss Delavie to her room, and showed herself much softened. As a good, conscientious woman, she felt that she had acted a selfish part towards the lonely maiden, and Betty's confident belief that she had been a kind friend was a keen reproach.

"Indeed, madam," she said, "I would lief you could truly call me such, but when young Miss came here first I took her for one of that flighty sort that it is wise not to meddle with more than needful. I have kept my place here these thirty years by never making or meddling, and knowing nothing about what don't concern me, and is out of my province. Now, I wish I had let the poor young lady be more friendly with me, for maybe I could have been of use to her in her need."

"You had no suspicion?"

"No, ma'am; though I find there were those who suspected some one came up here disguised as Jumbo; but I was never one to lend an ear to gossip, and by that time I trusted the dear young lady altogether, and knew she would never knowingly do aught that was unbecoming her station, or her religion."

"I am glad the dear child won your good opinion," said Betty.

"Indeed, ma'am, that you may say," returned Mrs. Aylward, whom anxiety had made confidential; "for I own I was prejudiced against her from the first, as, if you'll excuse me, ma'am, all we Bowstead people are apt to be set against whatever comes from my Lady's side. However, one must have been made of the nether millstone not to feel the difference she made in the house. She was the very life of it with her pretty ways, singing and playing with the children, and rousing up the poor gentleman too that had lived just like a mere heathen in a dungeon, and wouldn't so much as hear a godly word in his despair. And now he has a minister once a fortnight to read prayers, and is quite another man—all through that blessed young lady, who has brought him back to light and life." And as Betty's tears flowed at this testimony to her sister, the housekeeper added, "Never you fear, ma'am; she is one of God's innocents, and His Hand will be over her."

Meantime, having dismissed the young lover to take, if he could, a much needed night's rest, the Major was listening to Mr. Belamour's confession. " I was the most to blame, inasmuch as an old fool is worse than a young one ; and I would that the penalty fell on me alone."

"If she be in my cousin's hands I cannot believe that she will permit any harm to befall her," said the good Major, still clinging to his faith in Urania—the child he had taught to ride, and with whom he had danced her first minuet.

"What I dread most is her being forced into some low marriage," said Mr. Belamour. "The poor child's faith in the ceremony that passed must have been overthrown, and who can tell what she may be induced to accept?"

"It was that threat which moved you?" said the Major.

"Yes. Hargrave assured me that my Lady had actually offered her to him, with a bribe of a farm on easy terms ; and when she found that he had other intentions, there seemed to be some broken-down sycophant of Mar's upon the cards, but of course I was preferable, both because my fair sister-in law has some lingering respect for the honour of her own blood, and because the bar between Aurelia and my nephew would be perpetual. I knew likewise that it was my brother's earnest desire that a match should take place between your children and his."

"He did me too much honour. The lad showed me the extract from his letter."

"I could not give him the whole. It was fit for no eyes but mine, who had so long neglected it, and barely understood that it existed. My poor brother's eyes were fully opened to his wife's character, and even while he loved her to distraction, and yielded to her fascinating mastery against his better judgment, he left me the charge of trying in some degree to repair the injustice he believed you to be suffering, and of counteracting evil influences on her son."

"That seems at least to have been done."

"By no efforts of mine; but because the boy was happily permitted to remain with the worthy tutor his father had chosen for him, and because

Wayland is an excellent man, wise and prudent in all things save in being bewitched by a fair face. Would that he were returned! When I first consented to act this fool's part, I trusted that he would have been at home soon enough to prevent more than the nominal engagement, and when my Lady's threats rendered it needful to secure the poor child by giving her my name, I still expected him before my young gentleman should utterly betray himself by his warmth."

"He tells me that he has written."

"True. On that I insisted, and I am the more uneasy, for there has been ample time for a reply. It is only too likely, from what my nephew tells me of his venturesome explorations, that he may have fallen into the hands of the Moorish corsairs! Hargrave says it is rumoured; but my lady will not be checked in her career of pleasure, and if she is fearful of his return, she may precipitate matters with the poor girl!"

"Come, come, sir, I cannot have you give way to despondency. You did your best, and if it did not succeed, it was owing to my foolish daughter

Arden. Why, if she was not satisfied about her sister, could she not have come here, and demanded an explanation? That would have been the straightforward way!"

"Would that she had! Or would that I had sooner discovered my own entire recovery, which I owe in very truth to the sweet being who has brought new life alike of body and mind to me, and who must think I have requited her so cruelly."

CHAPTER VIII.

CYTHEREA'S BOWER.

> There Citherea goddesse was and quene,
> Honourid highly for her majestè,
> And eke her sonne, the mighty god I weene,
> Cupid the blinde, that for his dignitè
> A M lovers worshipp on ther kne.
> There was I bid on pain of dethe to pere,
> By Mercury, the wingèd messengere.—CHAUCER.

By twelve o'clock on the ensuing day Mr. Belamour, with Eugene and Jumbo, was set down at a hotel near Whitehall, to secure apartments, while the Major went on to demand his daughter from Lady Belamour, taking with him Betty, whom he allowed to be a much better match for my Lady than he could be. Very little faith in his cousin Urania remained to him in the abstract, yet even now he could not be sure that she would not talk him over and hoodwink him in any actual encounter. Sir Amyas likewise accompanied him, both to gratify his own anxiety and to secure admission. The young man still looked pale and worn with restless anxiety; but he had, in spite of remonstrances, that morning discarded his sling, saying that he should return to his quarters. Let his Colonel do his worst there; he had still more liberty than if compelled to return to his mother's house.

Lady Belamour had, on her second marriage, forsaken her own old hereditary mansion in the Strand, where Sir Jovian had died, and which, she said, gave her the vapours. Mr. Wayland, whose wealth far exceeded her own, had purchased one of the new houses in Hanover Square, the fashionable quarter and very much admired; but the Major regretted the gloomy dignity of the separate enclosure and walled court of Delavie House, whereas the new one, in modern fashion, had only an area and steps between the front and the pavement.

The hall door stood wide open, with a stately porter within, and lackeys planted about at intervals. Grey descended from the box, and after some inquiry, brought word that "her Ladyship was at breakfast," then, at a sign from his master, opened the carriage door. Sir Amyas, taking Betty by the tips of her fingers, led her forward, receiving by the way greetings and inquiries from the servants, whose countenances showed him to be a welcome arrival.

"Is it a reception day, Maine?" he asked of a kind of major-domo whom he met on the top of the broad stairs.

"No, your honour."

"Is company with her ladyship?"

"No, not company, sir," with a certain hesitation which damped Betty's satisfaction in the first assurance.

What did she see as Maine opened the door? It was a very spacious bedroom, the bed in an alcove hung with rose-coloured satin embroidered with myrtles and white roses, looped up with lace and muslin. Like draperies hung round the window, fluted silk lined the room, and beautiful japanned and inlaid cabinets and *étagères* adorned the walls, bearing all varieties and devices of new and old porcelain from China, Sèvres, Dresden, or Worcester, together with Moorish and Spanish curiosities, tokens of Mr. Wayland's travels. There was a toilette table before one window covered with lacquer ware, silver and ivory boxes, and other apparatus, and an exquisite Venetian mirror with the borders of frosted silver work.

Not far off, but sideways to it, sat Lady Belamour in a loose sacque of some rich striped silk, in crimson and blue stripes shot with gold threads. Slippers, embroidered with gold, showed off her dainty feet, and a French hairdresser stood behind her chair putting the finishing touches to the imposing fabric of powder, flower, and feather upon her head. A little hand-mirror, framed in carved ivory inlaid with coral, and a fan, lay on a tiny spindle-legged table close in front of her, together with a buff-coloured cup of chocolate. At a somewhat larger table Mrs. Loveday, her woman, was dispensing the chocolate, whilst a little negro boy, in a fantastic Oriental costume, waited to carry the cups about.

On a sofa near at hand, in an easy attitude, reclined Colonel Mar, holding out to Lady Belamour a snuff-box of tortoiseshell and gold, and a lady sat near on one of the tall black-and-gold chairs drinking chocolate, while all were giving their opinions on the laces, feathers, ribbons, and trinkets which another Frenchman was displaying from a basket-box placed on the floor, trying to keep aloof a little Maltese lion-dog, which had been roused from its cushion, and had come to inspect his wares. A little further off, Archer, in a blue velvet coat, white satin waistcoat, and breeches and silk stockings, and Amoret, white-frocked, blue-sashed, and bare-headed (an innovation of fashion), were admiring the nodding mandarins, grinning nondescript monsters, and green lions of extraordinary form which an emissary from a curiosity-shop was unpacking. Near the door, in an attitude weary yet obsequious, stood, paper in hand, a dejected figure in shabby plum-colour— *i.e.* a poor author—waiting in hopes that his sonnet in praise of Cytherea's triumphant charms would win him the guinea he so sorely needed, as

> To quench the blushes of ingenuous shame,
> And heap the shrine of luxury and pride
> With incense kindled at the Muses' flame.

The scene was completed by a blue and yellow macaw at one window chained to his perch, and a green monkey tethered in like manner at the other.

Of course Elizabeth Delavie did not perceive all these details at once. Her first sensation was the shock to the decorum of a modest English lady at intruding into a bed-room; but her foreign recollections coming to her aid, she accepted the fashion with one momentary feminine review of her own appearance, and relief that she had changed her travelling gear for her Sunday silks, and made her father put on his full uniform. All this passed while Sir Amyas was leading her into the room, steering her carefully out of the monkey's reach. Then he went a step or two forward and bent before his mother, almost touching the ground with one knee, as he kissed her hand, and rising, acknowledged the lady with a circular sweep of his hat, and his Colonel with a military salute, all rapidly, but with perfect ease and gracefulness. "Ah! my truant, my runaway invalid!" said Lady Belamour, "you are come to surrender."

"I am come," he said gravely, holding out his stronger hand to his little brother and sister, who sprang to him, "to bring my father- and sister-in-law, Major and Miss Delavie."

"Ah! my good cousin, my excellent Mrs. Betty, excuse me that my tyrant *friseur* prevents my rising to welcome you. It is so good and friendly in you to come in this informal way to cheer me under this terrible anxiety. Let me present you to my kind friend, the Countess of Aresfield, who has been so good as to come in to-day to sustain my spirits. Colonel Mar you know already. Pray be seated. Amyas—Archer—chairs. Let Syphax give you a cup of chocolate."

"Madam," said the Major, disregarding all this, and standing as if on parade, "can I see you alone? My business is urgent."

"No evil news, I trust! I have undergone such frightful shocks of late, my constitution is well nigh ruined."

"It is I that have to ask news of you, madam."

She saw that, if she trifled with him, something would break out that she would not wish to have said publicly. "My time is so little my own," she said, "I am under command to be at the Palace by two o'clock, but in a few minutes I shall be able to dismiss my tormentor, and then, till my woman comes to dress me, I shall be at your service. Sit down, I entreat, and take some chocolate. I know Mrs. Betty is an excellent housekeeper, and I want her opinion. My dear Lady Aresfield, suffer me to introduce my estimable cousin, Mrs. Betty Delavie."

The Countess, looking in her feathers and powder like a beetroot in white sauce, favoured Betty with a broad stare. Vulgarity was very vulgar in those days, especially when it had purchased rank, and thought manners might be dispensed with. Betty sat down, and Amoret climbed on her lap, while a diversion was made by Archer's imperious entreaty that his mamma would purchase a mandarin who not only nodded, but waved his hands and protruded his tongue.

Then ensued what seemed, to the sickening suspense of the two Delavies, a senseless Babel of tongues on all sides; but it ended in the *friseur* putting up his implements, the tradesfolk leaving the selected goods unpaid for, and the poor poet bowing himself within reach of the monkey, who made a clutch at his MS., chattered over it, and tore it into fragments. There was a peal of mirth—loudest from Lady Aresfield—but Sir Amyas sprang forward with gentlemanly regrets, apologies, and excuses, finally opening the door and following the poor man out of the room to administer the guinea from his own pocket, while Colonel Mar exclaimed, "Here, Archer, boy, run after him with this. The poor devil has won it by producing a smile from those divine lips— such as his jingle might never have done ——"

"Fie! fie! Mar," said the Lady, shaking her fan at him, " the child will repeat it to him."

" The better sport if he do," said Colonel Mar, carelessly ; " he may term himself a very Orpheus charming the beasts, so that they snatch his poems from him!"

Then, as Sir Amyas returned, Lady Belamour entreated her dear Countess to allow him to conduct her to the withdrawing room, and there endeavour to entertain her. The Colonel could not but follow, and the Major and Betty found themselves at length alone with her Ladyship.

"I trust you have come to relieve my mind as to our poor runaway," she began.

"Would to Heaven I could!" said the Major.

"Good Heavens! Then she has never reached you!"

"Certainly not."

"Nor her sister? Oh, surely she is with her sister!"

"No, madam, her sister knows nothing of her. Cousin, you have children of your own! I entreat of you to tell me what you have done with her."

"How should I have done anything with her? I who have been feeding all this time on the assurance that she had returned to you."

"How could a child like her do so?"

"We know she had money," said Lady Belamour.

"And we know," said Betty, fixing her eyes on the lady, "that though she escaped, on the first alarm, as far as Sedhurst, and was there seen, she had decided on returning to Bowstead and giving herself up to your Ladyship."

"Indeed? At what time was that?" exclaimed my Lady.

"Some time in the afternoon of Sunday!"

"Ah! then I must have left Bowstead. I was pledged to her Majesty's card-table, and royal commands cannot be disregarded, so I had to go away in grievous anxiety for my poor boy. She meant to return to Bowstead, did she? Ah! Does not an idea strike you that old Amyas Belamour may know more than he confesses? He has been playing a double game throughout."

"He is as anxious to find the dear girl as we are, madam."

"So he may seem to you and to my poor infatuated boy, but you see those crazed persons are full of strange devices and secrets, as indeed we have already experienced. I see what you would say; he may appear sane and plausible enough to a stranger, but to those who have known him ever since his misfortunes, the truth is but too plain. He was harmless enough as long as he was content to remain secluded in his dark chamber, but now that I hear he has broken loose, Heaven knows what mischief he may do. My dear cousin Delavie, you are the prop left to me in these troubles, with my poor good man in the hands of those cruel pirates, who may be making him work in chains for all I know," and the tears came into her beautiful eyes.

"They will not do that," said Major Delavie, eager to reassure her; "I have heard enough of their tricks to know that they keep such game as he most carefully till they can get a ransom."

"Your are sure of that!"

"Perfectly. I met an Italian fellow at Vienna who told me how it was all managed by the Genoese bankers."

"Ah! I was just thinking that you would be

the only person who could be of use—you who know foreign languages and all their ways. If you could go abroad, and arrange it for me!"

"If my daughter were restored ——" began the Major.

"I see what you would say, and I am convinced that the first step towards the discovery would be to put Mr. Belamour under restraint, and separate his black from him. Then one or other of them would speak, and we might know how she has been played upon."

"What does your Ladyship suppose then?" asked the Major.

"This is what I imagine. The poor silly maid repents herself and comes back in search of me. Would that she had found me, her best friend! But instead of that, she falls in with old Belamour, and he, having by this time perceived the danger of the perilous masquerade in which he had involved my unlucky boy, a minor, has mewed her up somewhere, till the cry should be over."

"That would be the part of a villain, but scarcely of a madman," said Betty dryly.

"My dear cousin Betty, there are lunatics endowed with a marvellous shrewdness to commit senseless villanies, and to put on a specious seeming. Depend upon it, my unfortunate brother-in-law's wanderings at night were not solely spent in communings with the trees and brooks. Who knows what might be discovered if he were under proper restraint? And it is to you, the only relation I have, that I must turn for assistance in my most unhappy circumstances," she added, with a glance so full of sweet helplessness that no man could withstand it. "I am so glad you are here. You will be acting for me as well as for yourself in endeavouring to find your poor lovely child, and the first thing I would have done would be to separate Belamour and his black, put them under restraint, and interrogate them separately. You could easily get an order from a magistrate. But ah, here comes my woman. No more now. You will come to me this evening, and we can talk further on this matter. I shall have some company, and it will not be a regular rout, only a few card-tables, and a little dancing for the young people."

"Your ladyship must excuse me," said Betty, "I have no dress to appear in, even if I had spirits for company."

"Ah! my dear cousin, how do you think it is with my spirits? Yet I think it my duty not to allow myself to be moped, but to exert myself for the interest of my son. While as to dress, my woman can direct you to a milliner who would equip you in the last mode. What, still obstinate? Nay, then, Harry, I can take no excuse from you, and I may have been able to collect some intelligence from the servants."

Nothing remained but to take leave and walk home, the Major observing—

"Well, what think you of that, Betty?"

"Think, sir?—I think it is not for my lady to talk of villains."

"She is in absolute error respecting Belamour; but then she has not seen him since his recovery. Women are prone to those fancies, and in her unprotected state, poor thing, no wonder she takes alarms."

"I should have thought her rather over-protected."

"Now, Betty, you need not take a leaf out of Mrs. Duckworth's book, and begin to be censorious. You saw how relieved she was to have me, her own blood relation, to turn to, instead of that empty braggart of a fellow. Besides, a man does not bring his step-mother when there's anything amiss."

There was something in this argument, and Betty held her peace, knowing that to censure my Lady only incited her father to defend her.

For her own part her consternation was great, and she walked on in silence, only speaking again to acquiesce in her father's observation that they must say nothing to Mr. Belamour of my Lady's plans for his seclusion.

They found Mr. Belamour in the square parlour of the Royal York, having sent Eugene out for a walk with Jumbo. The boy's return in the most eager state of excitement at the shops, the horses, sedans, and other wonders, did something, together with dinner, to wile away the weary time till, about three hours after the Major and his daughter had returned, they were joined by the young baronet, who came running up the stairs with a good deal more impetuosity than he would have permitted himself at home.

"At last I have escaped," he said. "I fear you have waited long for me?"

"I have been hoping you had discovered some indications," said the Major.

"Alas, no! I should imagine my Lady as ignorant as we are, save for one thing."

"And that was——?"

"The pains that were taken to prevent my speaking with any of the servants. I was forced to attend on that harridan, Lady Aresfield, till my mother sent for me; and then she made Mar absolutely watch me off the premises. Then I had to go and report myself at head-quarters, and see the surgeon, so that there may be no colour of irregularity for the Colonel to take advantage of."

"Right, right!" said the Major; "do not let

him get a handle against you, though I should not call you fit for duty yet, even for holiday-work like yours."

"You still suspect that your mother knows where our Aurelia is?" said Betty. "When I think of her demeanour, I can hardly believe it! But did you hear nothing of your little sisters?"

"I did not ask. In truth I was confounded by a proposal that was made to me. If I will immediately marry my mother's darling, Lady Belle, I may have leave of absence from her and my regiment, both at once, and go to meet Mr. Wayland if I like, or at any rate make the grand tour, while they try to break in my charming bride for me. Of course I said that, being a married man, nothing should induce me to break the law, nor to put any lady in such a position; and equally, of course, I was shown a lawyer's opinion that the transaction was invalid."

"As I always believed," said his uncle. "The ceremony must be repeated when we find her; though even if you were willing, the other parties are very ill-advised to press for a marriage without judgment first being delivered, how far the present is binding. So she wants to send you off on your travels, does she?"

"She wishes me to go and arrange for her husband's ransom," said the Major. "I would be ready enough were my child only found, but I believe government would take it up, he being on his Majesty's service."

"It is a mere device for disposing of you—yes, and of my nephew too," said Mr. Belamour. "As for me, we know already her kind plans for putting me out of reach of interference. I see, she communicated them to you. Did she ask your co-operation, Major? Ah! certainly, an ingenious plan for disuniting us. I am the more convinced that she is well aware of where the poor child is, and that she wishes to be speedy in her measures."

There is no need to describe the half-frantic vehemence of the young lover, nor the way in which the father and sister tried to moderate his transports, though no less wretched themselves.

CHAPTER IX.

THE ROUT.

> Great troups of people travelled thitherward
> Both day and night, of each degree and place.—SPENSER.

MUCH against their will, Major Delavie and his *soi-disant* son-in-law set forth for Lady Belamour's entertainment, thinking no opportunity of collecting intelligence was to be despised; while she probably wished to obviate all reports of a misunderstanding as well as to keep them under her own eye.

The reception rooms were less adorned than the lady's private apartment. There were pictures on the walls, and long ranks of chairs ranged round, and card-tables were set out in order. The ladies sat in rows, and the gentlemen stood in knots and talked, all in full dress, resplendent figures in brilliant velvet, gold lace, and embroidery, with swords by their sides, cocked hats, edged with gold or silver lace, under their arms, and gemmed shoe buckles. The order of creation was not yet reversed; the male creature was quite as gorgeous in colour and ornament as the female, who sat in her brocade, powder and patches, fan in hand, to receive the homage of his snuff-box.

Sir Amyas went the round, giving and returning greetings, which were bestowed on him with an ardour sufficient to prove that he was a general favourite. His mother, exquisitely dressed in a rich rose-coloured velvet train, over a creamy satin petticoat, both exquisitely embroidered, sailed up with a cordial greeting to her good cousin, and wanted to set him down to loo or ombre; but the veteran knew too well what the play in her house was, and saw, moreover, Lady Aresfield sitting like a harpy before the green baize field of her spoils. While he was refusing, Sir Amyas returned to him, saying, "Sir, here is a gentleman whom I think you must have known in Flanders;" and the Major found himself shaking hands with an old comrade.

Save for his heavy heart, he would have been extremely happy in the ensuing conversation.

In the meantime Lady Belamour, turning towards a stout, clumsy, short girl, her intensely red cheeks and huge black eyes staring out of her powder, while the extreme costliness of her crimson satin dress, and profusion of her rubies were ridiculous on the unformed person of a creature scarcely fifteen. If she had been any one else she would have been a hideous spectacle in the eyes of the exquisitely tasteful Lady Belamour, who, detecting the expression in her son's eye, whispered behind her fan, " We will soon set all that right;" then aloud, " My son cannot recover from his surprise. He did not imagine that we could steal you for an evening from Queen's Square to procure him this delight." Then as Sir Amyas bowed, " The Yellow Room is cleared for dancing. Lady Belle will favour you, Amyas."

"You must excuse me, madam," he said ; " I have not yet the free use of my arm, and could not acquit myself properly in a minuet."

"I hate minuets," returned Lady Belle; "the very notion gives me the spleen."

"Ah, pretty heretic!" said my Lady, making a playful gesture with her fan at the peony-coloured cheek. "I meant this wounded knight to have converted you, but he must amuse you otherwise. What, my Lord, I thought you knew I never meant to dance again. Cannot you open the dance without me? I, who have no spirits!"

The rest was lost as she sailed away on the arm of a gentleman in a turquoise-coloured coat, and waistcoat embroidered with gillyflowers; leaving the Lady Arabella on the hands of her son, who, neither as host nor gentleman, could escape, until the young lady had found some other companion. He stiffly and wearily addressed to her the inquiry how she liked London.

"I should like it monstrously if I were not moped up in school," she answered. "So you have come back. How did you hurt your arm?" she said, in the most provincial of dialects.

"In the fire, madam."

"What? In snatching your innamorata from the flames?"

"Not precisely," he said.

"Come, now, tell me; did she set the room a-fire?" demanded the young lady. "Oh, you need not think to deceive me. My brother Mar's coachman told my mamma's woman all about it, and how she was locked up and ran away; but they have her fast enough now, after all her tricks!"

"Who have? For pity's sake tell me, Lady Belle!"

Loving to tease, she exclaimed: "There, now, what a work to make about a white-faced little rustic!"

"Your ladyship has not seen her."

"Have I not, though? I don't admire your taste."

"Is she in Queen's Square?"

"Do not you wish me to tell you where you can find your old faded doll, with a waist just like a wasp, and an old blue sacque—not a bit of powder in her hair?"

"Lady Belle, if you would have me for ever beholden to you ——"

"The cap fits," she cried, clapping her hands. "Not a word to say for her! I would not have such a beau for the world."

"When I have found her it will be time to defend her beauty! If your ladyship would only tell me where she is, you know not what gratitude I should feel!"

"I dare say, but that's my secret. My mamma and yours would be ready to kill me with rage if they knew I had let out even so much."

"They would soon forgive you. Come, Lady Belle, think of her brave old father, and give some clue to finding her. Where is she?"

"Ah! where you will never get at her!"

"Is she at Queen's Square?"

"What would you do if you thought she was? Get a constable and come and search? Oh, what a rage Madam would be in! Goodness me, what sport!" and she fell back in a violent giggling fit; but the two matrons were so delighted to see the young people talking to one another, that there was no attempt to repress her. Sir Amyas made another attempt to elicit whether Aurelia were really at the school in Queen's Square, but Lady Arabella still refused to answer directly. Then he tried the expedient of declaring that she was only trying to tease him, and had not really seen the lady. He pretended not to believe her, but when she insisted, " Hair just the colour of Lady Belamour's," his incredulity vanished ; but on his next entreaty, she put on a sly look imitated from the evil world in which she lived, and declared she should not encourage naughty doings. The youth, who, though four years older, was by far the more simple and innocent of the two, replied with great gravity, " It is the Lady Belamour, my own wife, that I am seeking."

" That's just the nonsense she talks ! "

" For Heaven's sake, what did she say ? "

But Belle was tired of her game, and threw herself boisterously on a young lady who had the " sweetest enamel necklace in the world," and whose ornaments she began to handle and admire in true spoilt-child fashion.

Sir Amyas then betook himself to the Major, who saw at once by his eye and step that something was gained. They took leave together, Lady Belamour making a hurried lamentation that she had seen so little of her dear cousin, but accepting her son's excuse that he must return to his quarters; and they walked away together escorted by Palmer and Grey, as well as by two link-boys, summer night though it was.

Sir Amyas repaired first to the hotel, where Mr. Belamour and Betty were still sitting, for even the fashionable world kept comparatively early hours, and it was not yet eleven o'clock. The parlour where they sat was nearly dark, one candle out and the other shaded so as to produce the dimness which Mr. Belamour still preferred, and they were sitting on either side of the open window, Betty listening to her companion's reminiscences of the evenings enlivened by poor Aurelia, and of the many traits of her goodness, sweet temper, and intelligence which he had stored up in his mind. He had, he said, already learned through her to know Miss Delavie, and he declared that the voices of the sisters were so much alike that he could have believed himself at Bowstead with the gentle visitor who had brought him new life.

The tidings of Lady Arabella's secret were eagerly listened to, and the token of the mouse-coloured hair was accepted; Sir Amyas comparing, to every one's satisfaction, a certain lock that he bore on a chain next his heart, and a little knot, surrounded with diamonds, in a ring, which he had been still wearing from force of habit, though he declared he should never endure to do so again.

It was evident that Lady Belle had really seen Aurelia; and where could that have been save at the famous boarding-school in Queen's Square, where the daughters of " the great " were trained in the accomplishments of the day? The Major, with rising hopes, declared that he had always maintained that his cousin meant no ill by his daughter, and though it had been cruel, not to say worse, in her, to deny all knowledge of the fugitive, yet women would have their strange ways.

"That is very hard on us women, sir," said Betty.

"Ah! my dear, poor Urania never had such a mother as you, and she has lived in the great world besides, and that's a bad school. You will not take our Aurelia much into it, my dear boy," he added, turning wistfully to Sir Amyas.

"I would not let a breath blow on her that could touch the bloom of her charming frank innocence," cried the lad. "But think you she can be in health? Lady Belle spoke of her being pale!"

"Look at my young lady herself!" said the Major, which made them all laugh. They were full of hope. The Major and his daughter would go themselves the next day, and a father's claim could not be refused even though not enforced according to Lady Arabella's desire.

Their coach—for so Sir Amyas insisted on their going—was at the door at the earliest possible moment that a school for young ladies could be supposed to be astir; long before Mr. Belamour was up, for he retained his old habits so much that it was only on great occasions that he rose before noon; and while Eugene, under the care of Jumbo and Grey, was going off in great felicity to see the morning parade in St. James's Park.

One of the expedients of well-born Huguenot refugees had been tuition, and Madame d'Elmar had made her boarding-school so popular and fashionable that a second generation still maintained its fame, and damsels of the highest rank were sent there to learn French, to play the spinnet, to embroider, to dance, and to get into a carriage with grace. It was only countrified misses, bred by old-fashioned scholars, who attempted to go any farther, such as that *lusus naturæ*, Miss Elizabeth Carter, who knew seven languages, or the Bishop of Oxford's niece, Catherine Talbot, who even painted natural flowers and wrote meditations! The education Aurelia Delavie had received over her Homer and Racine would be smiled at as quite superfluous.

There was no difficulty about admission. The coach with its Belamour trappings was a warrant of admittance. The father and daughter were shown into a parlour with a print of Marshal Schomberg over the mantelpiece, and wonderful performances in tapestry work and embroidery on every available chair, as well as framed upon the wainscoted walls.

A little lady, more French than English, moving like a perfectly wound up piece of mechanism, all but her bright little eyes, appeared at their request to see Madame. It had been agreed beforehand that the Major should betray neither doubt nor difficulty, but simply say that he had come up from the country and wished to see his daughter.

Madame, in perfectly good English, excused herself, but begged to hear the name again.

There must be some error, no young lady of the name of Delavie was there.

They looked at one another, then Betty asked, "Has not a young lady been placed here by Lady Belamour?"

"No, madam, Lady Belamour once requested me to receive her twin daughters, but they were mere infants; I receive none under twelve years old."

"My good lady" cried the Major, "if you are denying my daughter to me, pray consider what you are doing. I am her own father, and whatever Lady Belamour may tell you, I can enforce my claim."

"I am not in the habit of having my word doubted, sir," and the little lady drew herself up like a true Gascon baroness, as she was.

"Madam, forgive me, I am in terrible perplexity and distress. My poor child, who was under Lady Belamour's charge, has been lost to us these three weeks or more, and we have been told that she has been seen here."

"Thus," said Betty, seeing that the lady still needed to be appeased, "we thought Lady Belamour might have deceived you as well as others."

"May I ask who said the young lady had been seen here?" asked the mistress coldly.

"It was Lady Arabella Mar," said Betty, "and, justly speaking, I believe she did not say it was here that my poor sister was seen, but that she had seen her, and we drew the conclusion that it was here."

"My Lady Arabella Mar is too often taken out by my Lady Countess," said Madame d'Elmar.

"Could I see her? Perhaps she would tell me where she saw my dear sister?" said Betty.

"She went to a rout last evening and has not returned," was the reply. "Indeed my lady, her mother, spoke as if she might never come back, her marriage being on the *tapis*. Indeed, sir, indeed, madam, I should most gladly assist you," she said, as a gesture of bitter grief and disappointment passed between father and daughter, both of whom were evidently persons of condition. "If it will be any satisfaction to the lady to see all my pupils, I will conduct her through my establishment."

Betty caught at this, though there was no doubt that the mistress was speaking in good faith. She was led to a large empty room, where a dozen young ladies were drawn up awaiting the dancing master—girls from fourteen to seventeen, the elder ones in mob caps, those with more pretensions to fashion, with loose hair. Their twelve curtsies were made, their twenty-four eyes peeped more or less through their lashes at the visitor, but no such soft brown eyes as Aurelia's were among them.

"Madame," said Betty, "may I be permitted to

ask the young ladies a question?" She spoke it low, and in French, and her excellent accent won Madame's heart at once. Only Madame trusted to Mademoiselle's discretion not to put mysteries into their minds, or they would be all *tête montée*.

So, as discreetly as the occasion would permit, Betty asked whether any one had seen or heard Lady Belle speak of having seen any one—a young girl—a young lady?

Half-a-dozen tongues broke out, "We thought it all Lady Belle's whimsical secrets," and as many stories were beginning, but Madame's awful little hand waved silence, as she said, "Speak then, Miss Staunton."

"I know none of Lady Belle's secrets, ma'am—ask Miss Howard."

Miss Howard looked sulky; and a little eager, black-eyed thing cried, "She said it was an odious girl whom Lady Belamour keeps shut up in a great dungeon of an old house, and is going to send beyond seas, because she married two men at once in disguise."

"Fie, Miss Crawford, you know nothing about it."

"You told me so, yourself, Miss Howard."

"I never said anything so foolish."

"Hush, young ladies," said Madame. "Miss Howard, if you know anything, I request you to speak."

"It would be a great kindness," said Betty. "Might I ask the favour of seeing Miss Howard in private?"

Madame consented, and Miss Howard followed Betty out of hearing, muttering that Belle would fly at her for betraying her.

"I do not like asking you to betray your friend's confidence," said Betty gently.

"Oh, as to that, I'm not her friend, and I believe she has talked to half-a-dozen more."

"I am this poor young lady's sister," said Betty. "We are afraid she has fallen into unkind hands; and I should be very thankful if you could help me to find her. Where do you think Lady Belle saw her?"

"I thought it was in some old house in Hertfordshire," said Miss Howard, more readily, "but I am not sure; for it was last Sunday, which she spent with her mamma. She came back and made it a great secret that she had seen the girl that had taken in Sir Amyas Belamour, who was contracted to herself, to marry him and his uncle both at once in disguise, and then had set the house a-fire. Belle had got some one to let her see the girl, and then she went on about her being not pretty."

"What did she say about sending her beyond seas?"

"Oh! that Miss Crawford made up. She told me that they were going to find a husband for her such as a low creature like that deserved. And she protests she is to be married to Sir Amyas very soon, and come back here while he makes the grand tour. I hope she won't. She will have more spiteful ways than ever."

This was all that Betty could extract. She saw Miss Crawford alone, but her tidings melted into the vaguest second-hand hearsay. The inquiry had only produced a fresh anxiety.

CHAPTER X.

A BLACK BLONDEL.

*And to the castle gate approached in quiet wise,
Whereat soft knocking, entrance he desired.*
                              SPENSER.

"NEPHEW, is Delavie House inhabited?" inquired Mr. Belamour, as the baffled seekers sat together that evening.

"No, sir," replied Sir Amyas. "My Lady will only lease it to persons of quality, on such high terms that she cannot obtain them for a house in so antiquated a neighbourhood. Oh, you do not think it possible that my dearest life can be in captivity so near us! An old house! On my soul, so it must be; I will go thither instantly."

"And be taken for a Mohock! No, no, sit down, rash youth, and tell me who keeps the house."

"One Madge, an old woman as sour as vinegar, who snarled at me like a toothless cur when I once went there to find an old fowling-piece of my father's."

"Then you are the last person who should show yourself there, since there are sure to be strict charges against admitting you, and you would only put the garrison on the alert. You had better let the reconnoitring party consist of Jumbo and myself."

The ensuing day was Sunday. Something was said of St. Paul's, then in the bloom of youth and the wonder of England; but Betty declared that she could not run about to see fine churches till her mind was at ease about her poor sister. Might she only go to the nearest and quietest church? So she, with her father and Eugene, repaired to St. Clement Danes, where their landlord possessed a solid oak pew, and they heard a sermon on the wickedness and presumption of inoculating for the small-pox.

It was not a genteel neighbourhood, and the congregation was therefore large, for the substantial tradesfolk who had poured into the Strand since it had been rebuilt were far more religiously disposed than the fashionable world, retaining either the Puritan zeal, or the High Church fervour, which were alike discouraged in the godless court. The Major and his son and daughter were solitary units in the midst of the groups of portly citizens, with soberly handsome wives, and gay sons and daughters, who were exchanging greetings; and on their return to their hotel, the Major betook himself to a pipe in the bar, and Eugene was allowed to go for a walk in the park with Palmer, while Betty sat in her own room with her Bible, striving to strengthen her assurance that the innocent would never be forsaken. Indeed Mr. Belamour had much strengthened her grounds of hope and comfort by his testimony to poor Aurelia's perfect guilelessness and simplicity throughout the affair. Yet the echo of that girl's chatter about Lady Belle's rival being sent beyond sea would return upon her ominously, although it might be mere exaggeration and misapprehension, like so much besides.

A great clock, chiming one, warned her to repair to the sitting-room, where she met Eugene, full of the unedifying spectacle of a fight between two street lads. There had been a regular ring, and the boy had been so much excited that Palmer had had much ado to bring him away. Betty had scarcely hushed his eager communications and repaired his toilette for dinner before Sir Amyas came in, having hurried away as soon as possible after attending his men to and from church.

"Sister," he said, for so he insisted on calling Betty, "I really think my uncle's surmise may be right. I went home past Delavie House last night, just to look at it, and there was—there really was, a light in one of the windows on the first floor, which always used to be as black as Erebus. I had much ado to keep myself from thundering at the gate. I would have done so before now but for my uncle's warning. Where can he be?"

The Major and Mr. Belamour here came in together, and the same torrent was beginning to be poured forth, when the latter cut it short with, "They are about to lay the cloth. Restrain yourself, my dear boy, or——" and as at that moment the waiter entered, he went on with the utmost readiness—"or, as it seems, the Queen of Hungary will never make good her claims. Pray, sir," turning to Major Delavie, "have you ever seen these young Archduchesses whose pretensions seem likely to convulse the continent to its centre?"

The Major, with an effort to gather his attention, replied that he could not remember; but Betty, with greater presence of mind, described how she had admired the two sisters of Austria as little girls walking on the Prater. Indeed she and Mr. Belamour contrived to keep up the ball till the Major was roused into giving an opinion of Prussian discipline, and to tell stories of Leopold of Dessau, Eugene, and Marlborough with sufficient zest to drive the young baronet almost frantic, especially as Jumbo, behind his master's chair, was on the broad grin all the time, and almost dancing in his shoes. Once he contrived to give an absolute wink with one of his big black eyes; not, however, undetected, for Mr. Belamour in a grave tone of reprimand ordered him off to fetch an ivory toothpick-case.

Not till the cloth had been removed, and dishes of early strawberries and of biscuits, accompanied by bottles of port and claret, placed on the table, and the servants had withdrawn, did Mr. Belamour observe, " I have penetrated the outworks."

There was an outburst of inquiry and explanation, but he was not to be prevented from telling the story in his own way. "I know the house well, for my brother lived there the first years of his marriage, before you came on the stage, young sir. Perhaps you do not know how to open the door from without?"

" Oh, sir, tell me the trick!"

Mr. Belamour held up a small pass-key. There was a certain tone of banter about him which almost drove his nephew wild, but greatly reassured Miss Delavie.

" Why—why keep me in torments, instead of taking me with you?" cried the youth.

"Because I wished my expedition to be no failure. I could not tell whether my key, which I found with my watch and seals, would still serve me. Ah! you look on fire; but remember the outworks are not the citadel."

"For Heaven's sake, sir, torture me not thus!"

"I knew that to make my summons at the outer gate would lead to a summary denial by the sour porteress, so I experimented on the lock of the little door into the lane, and admitted myself and Jumbo into the court; but the great hall-door stood before me jealously closed, and the lower windows were shut with shutters, so that all I could do was to cause Jumbo to awake the echoes with a lusty peal on the knocker, which he repeated at intervals, until there hobbled forth to open it a crone as wrinkled and crabbed as one of Macbeth's witches. I demanded whether my Lady Belamour lived there. She croaked forth a negative sound, and had nearly shut the door in my face, but I kept her in parley by protesting that I had often visited my Lady there, and offering a crown-piece if she would direct me to her."

"A crown! a kingdom, if she would bring us to the right one!" cried Sir Amyas.

"Of course she directed me to Hanover Square, and then, evidently supposing there was something amiss with the great gates, she insisted on coming to let me out, and securing them after me."

The youth gave a great groan, saying, "Excuse me, sir, but what are we the better of that?"

"Endure a little while, impatient swain, and you shall hear. I fancy she recognised the Belamour livery on Jumbo, for she hobbled by my side maundering apologies about its being against orders to admit gentle or simple, beast or body into the court, and that a poor woman could not lose her place and the roof over her head. But mark me, while this was passing, Jumbo, who had kept nearer the house, whistling 'The Nightingale' just above his breath, heard his name called, and presently saw two little faces at an up-stairs window."

"My little sisters!" cried Sir Amyas.

"Even so; and he believes he heard one of them call out, 'Cousin, cousin Aura, come and see Jumbo;' but as the window was high up, I scarce dare credit his ears rather than his imagination, and we were instantly hustled away by the old woman, whose evident alarm is a further presumption that the captive is there, since Faith and Hope scarce have reached the years of being princesses immured in towers."

"It must be so," said Betty; "it would explain Lady Belle's having had access to her! And now?"

"Is it impossible to effect an entrance from the court and carry her away?" asked Sir Amyas.

"Entirely so," said his uncle. "The only door into the court is fit to stand a siege, and all the lower windows are barred and fastened with shutters. The servants' entrance is at the back towards the river, but no doubt it is also guarded, and my key will not serve for it."

"I could get some sprightly fellows of ours to come disguised as Mohocks, and break in," proceeded the youth, eagerly. "Once in the court, trust me for forcing my way to her."

"And getting lodged in Newgate for your pains, or tried by court-martial," said the Major. "No, when right is on our side, do not let us make it wrong. Hush, Sir Amyas, it is I who must here act. Whether you are her husband I do not know, I know that I am her father, and to-morrow morning, as soon as a magistrate can be spoken with, I shall go and demand a search warrant for the body of my daughter, Aurelia Delavie."

"The body! Good Heavens, sir," cried Betty.

"Not without the sweet soul, my dear Miss Delavie," said Mr. Belamour. "Your excellent father has arrived at the only right and safe decision, and provided no farther alarm is given, I think he may succeed. It is scarcely probable that my Lady is in constant communication with her stern porteress, and my person was evidently unknown. For her own sake, as well as that of the small fee I dropped into her hand, she is unlikely to report my reconnoissance."

Sir Amyas was frantic to go with his father-in-law, but both the elder men justly thought that his ambiguous claims would but complicate the matter. The landlord was consulted as to the acting magistrates of the time, and gave two or three addresses.

Another night of prayer, suspense, and hope

for Betty's sick heart. Then, immediately after breakfast, the Major set forth, attended by Palmer, long before Mr. Belamour had left his room, or the young baronet could escape from his military duties. Being outside the City, the Strand was under the jurisdiction of justices of the peace for Middlesex, and they had so much more than they could do properly, that some of them did it as little as possible. The first magistrate would not see him, because it was too early to attend to business; the second never heard matters at his private house, and referred him to the office in Bow Street. In fact he would have been wiser to have gone thither at first, but he had hoped to have saved time. He had to wait sitting on a greasy chair when he could no longer stand, till case after case was gone through, and when he finally had a hearing and applied for a warrant to search for his daughter in Delavie House, there was much surprise and reluctance to put such an insult on a lady of quality in favour at Court. On his giving his reasons on oath for believing the young lady to be there, the grounds of his belief seemed to shrink away, so that the three magistrates held consultation whether the warrant could be granted. Finally, after eying him all over, and asking him where he had served, one of them, who had the air of having been in the army, told him that in consideration of his being a gentleman of high respectability who had served his country, they granted what he asked, being assured that he would not make the accusation lightly. The reforms made by Fielding had not yet begun, everybody had too much work, and the poor Major had still some time to wait before an officer—tipstaff, as he was called—could accompany him, so that it was past noon when, off in the Bowstead carriage again, they went along the Strand, to a high-walled court belonging to one of the old houses of the nobility, most of which had perished in the fire of London. There was a double-doored gateway, and after much thundering in vain, at which the tipstaff, a red-nosed old soldier, waxed very irate, the old woman came out in curtseying, crying, frightened humility, declaring that they would find no one there—they might look if they would.

So they drove over the paved road, crossing the pitched pebbles, the door was unbarred, but no Aurelia sprang into her father's arms. Only a little terrier came barking out into the dismal paved hall. Into every room they looked, the old woman asseverating denials that it was of no use, they might see for themselves, that no one had been there for years past. Full of emptiness, indeed, with faded grimy family portraits on the walls, moth-eaten carpets and cushions, high-backed chairs with worm-holes; and yet, somehow, there was one room that did look as if it had recently been sat in. Two little stools were drawn up close to a chair; the terrier poked and smelt about uneasily as though in search of some one, and dragged out from under a couch a child's ball which he began to worry. On the carpet, too, were some fragments of bright fresh embroidery silk, which the practised eye of the constable noticed. "This here was not left ten or a dozen years ago," said he; and, extracting the ball from the fangs of the dog, "No, and this ball ain't ten year old, neither. Come, Mother What's'-name, it's no good deceiving an officer of the law ; whose is this here ball?"

"It's the little misses. They've a bin here with their maid, but their nurse have been and fetched 'em away this morning, and a good riddance too."

"Who was the maid?—on your oath!"

"One Deborah Davis, a deaf woman, and pretty nigh a dumb one. She be gone too."

Nor could the old woman tell where she was to be found. "My Lady's woman had sent her in," she said, "and she was glad enough to be rid of her."

"Come, now, my good woman, speak out, and it will be better for you," said the Major. "I know my daughter was here yesterday."

"And what do I know of where she be gone? She went off in a sedan-chair this morning before seven o'clock, and if you was to put me to the rack I couldn't say no more."

As to which way or with whom she had gone, the old woman was, apparently, really ignorant.

The poor Major had to return home baffled and despairing, still taking the tipstaff with him, in case, on consultation with Mr. Belamour, it should be deemed expedient to storm Hanover Square itself, and examine Lady Belamour and her servants upon oath.

Behold, the parlour was empty. Even Betty and Eugene were absent. The Major hastened to knock at Mr. Belamour's door. There was no answer; and when he knocked louder it was still in vain. He tried the door and found it locked. Then he retreated to the sitting-room, rang, and made inquiries of the waiter who answered the bell.

Mr. Belamour had received a note at about ten o'clock, and had gone out with his servant. Sir Amyas Belamour had shortly after come very hastily to the parlour, and Miss Delavie and the little master had gone out with him " in great disorder," said the waiter.

At the same moment there was a knock at the door, and a billet was brought in from Lady Belamour. The Major tore it open and read:—

"My dear Cousin,

"I grieve for you, but my Suspicions were correct. We have all been completely hoodwinked by that old Villain, my Brother-in-law. I can give him no other Name, for his partial Aberration of Mind has only sharpened his natural Cunning. Would you believe it? He had obtained access to Delavie House, and had there hidden the unfortunate Object of your Search, while he pretended to be assisting you, and this Morning he carried her off in a Sedan. I have sent the good Doves to Bowstead in case he should have the Assurance to return to his old Quarters, but I suspect that they are on the Way to Dover. You had better consult with Hargrave on the means of confirming the strange Marriage Ceremony that has passed between them, since that affords the best Security for your Daughter's Maintenance and Reputation. Believe me, I share in your Distress. Indeed I have so frightful a Megrim that I can scarcely tell what I write, and I dare not admit you to-day.

"I remain,

"Your loving and much-grieved Cousin,

"URANIA BELAMOUR"

Poor Major! His horror, perplexity, and despair were indescribable. He had one only hope—that Sir Amyas and Betty might be on the track.

CHAPTER XI.

THE FIRST TASK.

> After all these there marcht a most faire dame,
> Led of two gryslie villains, th' one Despight,
> The other cleped Crueltie by name.
> SPENSER.

THE traces of occupation had not deceived Major Delavie; Aurelia had been recently in Delavie House, and we must go back some way in our narrative to describe her arrival there.

She had, on her return from Sedhurst on that Sunday, reached Bowstead, and entered by the lobby door just as Lady Belamour was coming down the stairs only attended by her woman, and ready to get into the carriage which waited at the hall door.

Sinking on her knees before her with clasped hands, Aurelia exclaimed, "O madam, I ought not to have come away. Here I am, do what you will with me, but spare my father. He knew nothing of it. Only, for pity's sake, do not put me among the poor wicked creatures in gaol."

"Get into that carriage immediately, and you shall know my decision," said Lady Belamour, with icy frigidness, but not the same fierceness as before; and Aurelia submissively obeyed, silenced by an imperious gesture when she would have asked, "How is it with *him?*" whom she durst not name.

Lady Belamour waited a minute or two while sending Loveday on a last message to the sick room, then entered the large deep carriage, signing to her captive to take a corner where she could hardly be seen if any one looked through the window. Loveday followed, the door was shut by a strange servant, as it was in fact Lady Aresfield's carriage, borrowed both for the sake of speed, and of secrecy towards her own household.

A few words passed by which Aurelia gathered something reassuring as to the state of the patient, and then Lady Belamour turned on her, demanding, "So, young miss, you tried to escape me! Where have you been?"

"Only as far as Sedhurst Church, madam. I would have gone home, but I feared to bring trouble on my father, and I came back to implore you to forgive."

There was no softening of the terrible, beautiful face before her, and she durst put no objective case to her verb. However, the answer was somewhat less dreadful than she had anticipated.

"I have been shamefully duped," said Lady Belamour, "but it is well that it is no worse; nor shall I visit your offences on your father if you show your penitence by absolute submission. The absurd ceremony you went through was a mere mockery, and the old fool, Belamour, showed himself crazed for consenting to such an improper frolic on the part of my son. Whether your innocence be feigned or not, however, I cannot permit you to go out of my custody until the foolish youth or yourself be properly bestowed in marriage elsewhere. Meantime, you will remain where I place you, and exactly fulfil my commands.

Remember that any attempt to communicate with any person outside the house will be followed by your father's immediate dismissal."

"May I not let him know that I am safe?"

"Certainly not; I will see to your father."

It was a period when great ladies did not scruple to scold at the top of their voices, and sometimes proceed to blows, but Lady Belamour never raised her low silvery tones, and thus increased the awfulness of her wrath and the impressiveness of her determination. Face to face with her, there were few who did not cower under her displeasure; and poor Aurelia, resolute to endure for her father's sake, could only promise implicit obedience.

She only guessed when they entered London by the louder rumbling, and for one moment the coach paused as a horse was reined up near it, and with plumed hat in hand the rider bent forward to the window, exclaiming, "Successful, by all that is lovely! Captured, by Jove!"

"You shall hear all another time," said Lady Belamour. "Let us go on now."

They did so, but the horseman continued to

flash across the windows, and when the coach, after considerable delay, had entered the walled court, rumbled over the pavement, and stopped before a closed door, he was still there. When, after much thundering, the door was opened, Aurelia had a moment's glimpse of a splendid figure in gold and scarlet handing out Lady Belamour, who stood talking with him on the steps of the house for some moments. Then, shrugging his shoulders, he remounted, and cantered off, after which my Lady signed to Aurelia to alight, and followed her into the hall.

"Madge," said Lady Belamour to the witch-like old woman who had admitted her, "this young lady is to remain here. You will open a bedroom and sitting-room for her at the back of the house. Let her be properly cared for, and go out in the court behind, but on no account approach the front gates. Let no one know she is here."

Madge muttered some demands about supplies and payments, and Lady Belamour waved her to settle them with Mrs. Loveday, turning meantime to the prisoner and saying, "There, child, you are to remain here on your good behaviour. Do your best to merit my good will, so that I may overlook what is past. Recollect, the least attempt to escape, or to hold intercourse with the young, or the old, fool, and it shall be the worse with them and with your father."

Therewith she departed, followed by Loveday, leaving Aurelia standing in the middle of the hall, the old hag gazing on her with a malignant leer. "Ho! ho! So that's the way! He has begun that work early, has he? What's your name, my lass? Oh, you need give yourself airs! I cry you mercy," and she made a derisive curtsey.

Poor Aurelia, pride had less to do with her silence than absolute uncertainty what to call herself. The wedding ring was on her finger, and she would not deny her marriage by calling herself Delavie, but Belamour might be dangerous, and the prefix was likewise a difficulty, so faltered "You may call me Madam Aurelia."

"Madam Really. That's a queer name, but it will serve while you are here."

"Pray let me go to my room," entreated the

poor prisoner, who felt an ineffable disgust at her jailor, and was becoming sensible to extreme fatigue.

"Your room, hey? D'ye think I keep rooms and beds as though this were an inn, single-handed as I am? You must wait, unless you be too fine to lend a hand."

"Anything will do," said Aurelia, "if I may only rest. I would help, but I am so much tired that I can hardly stand."

"My Lady has given it to you well, Mistress Really or Mistress Falsely, which ever you may be," mumbled Madge, perhaps in soliloquy, fumbling at the lock of a room which at last she opened. It smelt very close and fusty, and most of the furniture was heaped together under a cloth in the midst, dimly visible by the light of a heart-shaped aperture in the shutters. Unclosing one of the leaves, the old woman admitted enough daylight to guide Aurelia to a couch against the wall, saying, "You can wait there till I see to your bed. And you'll be wanting supper too!" she added in a tone of infinite disgust.

"O never mind supper, if I can only go to bed," sighed Aurelia, sinking on the couch as the old woman hobbled off. Lassitude and exhaustion had brought her to a state like annihilation—unable to think or guess, hope or fear, with shoes hurting her footsore feet, a stiff dress cramping her too much for sleep, and her weary aching eyes gathering a few impressions in a passive way. On the walls hung dimly seen portraits strangely familiar to her. The man in a green dressing gown with floating hair had a face she knew; so had the lady in the yellow ruff. And was not that the old crest, the Delavie butterfly, with the motto, *Ma Vie et ma Mie*, carved on the mantelpiece? Thus she knew that she must be in Delavie House, and felt somewhat less desolate as she recognised several portraits as duplicates of those at the Great House at Carminster, and thought they looked at her in pity with their eyes like her father's. The youngest son in the great family group was, as she knew, an Amyas, and he put her in mind of her own. Oh, was he her own, when she could not tell whether those great soft, dark-grey eyes that looked so kindly on her had descended to the young baronet? She hoped not, for Harriet and she had often agreed that they presaged the fate of that gallant youth, who had been killed by Sir Bevil Grenville's side. He must have looked just as Sir Amyas did, lying senseless after the hurt she had caused.

No more definite nor useful thoughts passed through the brain of the overwearied maiden as she rested on the couch, how long she knew not; but it was growing dark by the time Madge returned with a guttering candle, a cracked plate and wedge of greasy-looking pie, a piece of dry bread, a pewter cup of small beer, and an impaired repulsive steel knife with a rounded end, and fork with broken prong. The fact of this being steel was not distressing to one who had never seen a silver fork, but the condition of both made her shudder, and added to the sick sense of exhaustion that destroyed her appetite. She took a little of the bread, and, being parched with thirst, drank some of the sour beer before Madge came back again. "Oh ho, you're nice I see, my fine Dame Really!"

"Thank you, indeed I can't eat, I am so much tired," said Aurelia apologetically.

"You'll have to put up with what serves your betters, I can tell you," was all the reply she received. "Well, be ye coming to your bed?"

So up the creaking stairs she was guided to a room, very unlike that fresh white bower at Bowstead, large, eerie, ghostly-looking, bare save for a dark oak chest, and a bed of the same material, the posts apparently absolute trees, squared and richly carved, and supporting a solid wooden canopy with an immense boss as big as a cabbage, and carved something like one, depending from the centre, as if to endanger the head of the unwary, who should start up in bed. No means of ablution were provided, and Aurelia felt so grimed and dusty that she ventured to beg for an ewer and basin; but her amiable hostess snarled out that she had enough to do without humouring fiddle-faddle whimsies, and that she might wash at the pump if nothing else would serve her.

Aurelia wished she had known this before going up stairs, and, worn out as she was, the sense implanted by her mother that it was wicked to go to sleep dirty, actually made her drag herself down to a grim little scullery, where she was permitted to borrow a wooden bowl, since she was too *nice* forsooth to wash down stairs. She carried it up with considerable trouble more than half full, and a bit of yellow soap and clean towel were likewise vouchsafed to her. The wash—perhaps because of the infinite trouble it cost her—did her great good,—it gave her energy to recollect her prayers and bring good angels about her. If this had been her first plunge from home, when Jumbo's violin had so scared her, such a place as this would have almost killed her; but the peace that had come to her in Sedhurst Church lingered still round her, and as she climbed up into the lofty bed the verse sang in her ears "Love is strong as death." Whether Love Divine or human she did not ask herself, but with the sense of soothing upon her, she slept—and slept as a seventeen-years'-old frame will sleep after having been thirty-six hours awake and afoot.

When she awoke it was with the sense of some one being in the room. "O gemini!" she heard, and starting up, only just avoiding the knob, she saw Mrs. Loveday's well-preserved brunette face gazing at her.

"Your servant, ma'am," she said. "You'll excuse me if I speak with you here, for I must be back by the time my Lady's bell rings."

"Is it very late?" said Aurelia, taking from under her pillow her watch, which had stopped long ago.

"Nigh upon ten, o'clock," said Loveday. "I must not stay, but it is my Lady's wish that you should have all that is conformable, and you'll let me know how Madge behaves herself."

"Is there any news from Bowstead?" was all Aurelia could at first demand.

"Not yet; but bless you, my dear young lady, you had best put all that matter out of your head for ever and a day. I know what these young gentlemen are. They are not to be hearkened to one moment, not the best of them. Let them be ever so much in earnest at the time, their parents and guardians have the mastery of them sooner or later, and the farther it has gone, the worse it is. I saw you lying asleep here looking so innocent that it went to my heart, and I heard you mutter in your sleep 'Love is strong as death,' but that's only a bit of some play-book, and don't you trust to it, for I never saw love that was stronger than a spider's web."

"Oh, hush, Mrs. Loveday. It is in the Bible!"

"You don't say so, ma'am," the woman said awestruck.

"I would show it you, only all my things are away. God is love, you know," said Aurelia, sitting up with clasped hands, "and He gives it, so it must be strong."

"Well, all the love I've ever seen was more the devil's," said Loveday truly enough; "and you'll find it so if you mean to trust to these fine young beaux and what they say."

Aurelia shook her head a little as she sat up in

bed with her clasped hands; and there was a look on her face that Mrs. Loveday did not understand, as she went on with her advice.

"So, my dear young lady, you see all that is left for you is to frame your mind to keep close here, and conform to my Lady's will till all is blown over one way or another."

"I know that," said Aurelia.

"Don't you do anything to anger her," added the waiting-woman, "for there's no one who can stand against her; and I'll speak up for you when I can, for I know how to come round my Lady, if any one does. Tell me what you want, and I'll get it for you; but don't try to get out, and don't send Madge, for she is not to be trusted with money. If I were you, I'd not let her see that watch, and I'd lock my door at night. You're too innocent, whatever my Lady may say. Here's half a pound of tea and some sugar, which you had best keep to yourself, and I've seen to there being things decent down stairs. Tell me, my dear, is there anything you want. Your clothes, did you say? Oh, yes, you shall have them—yes, and your books. Here's some warm water," as a growling was heard at the door; "I must not wait till you are dressed, but there's a box of shells down in your room that Mr. Wayland sent home for my Lady to line a grotto with, and she wants them all sorted out. 'Tell her she must make herself of use if she wants to be forgiven,' says my Lady, for she is in a mighty hurry for them now she has heard of the Duchess of Portland's grotto, though she has let them lie here unpacked for this half year and more. So if they are all done by night, maybe my Lady will be pleased to let you have a bit more liberty."

Mrs. Loveday departed, having certainly cheered the captive, and Aurelia rose, weary-limbed and sad-hearted, with a patient trust in her soul that Love Divine would not fail her, and that earthly love would do its best.

She found matters improved in the down-stairs room, the furniture was in order, a clean cloth on the table, a white roll, butter, and above all clean bright implements, showing Mrs. Loveday's influence. She ate and drank like a hungry girl, washed up for herself rather than let Madge touch anything she could help, and looked from the window into a dull court of dreary, blighted-looking turf divided by flagged walks, radiating from a statue in the middle, representing a Triton blowing a conch—no doubt intended to spout water, for there was a stone trough round him, but he had long forgotten his functions, and held a sparrow's nest with streaming straws in his hand. This must be the prison-yard, where alone she might walk, since it lay at the back of the house; and with a sense of depression she turned to the task that awaited her.

A very large foreign-looking case had been partly opened, and when she looked in she was appalled at the task to be accomplished in one day. It was crammed with shells of every size and description, from the large helmet-conch and Triton's trumpet, down to the tiny pink cowry and rice-volute, all stuffed together without arrangement or packing, forming a mass in which the unbroken shells reposed in a kind of sand, of *débris* ground together out of the victims; and when she took up a tolerably-sized univalve, quantities of little ones came tumbling out of its inner folds. She took up a handful, and presently picked out one perfect valve like a rose petal, three fairy cups of limpets, four ribbed cowries, and a thing like a green pea. Of course she knew no names, but a kind of interest was awakened by the beauty and variety before her. A pile of papers had been provided, and the housewife which Betty made her always carry in her pocket furnished wherewithal to make up a number of bags for the lesser sorts; and she went to work, her troubles somewhat beguiled by the novel beauties of each delicate creature she disinterred, but remembering with a pang how, if she could have described them to Mr. Belamour, he would have discoursed upon the Order of Nature.

London noises were not the continuous roar of vehicles of the present day, but there was sound enough to remind the country girl where she was, and the street cries "Old Clothes!" "Sprats, oh!" "Sweep!" were heard over the wall, sometimes with tumultuous voices that seemed to enhance her loneliness, as she sat on the floor, hour after hour, sifting out the entire shells, and feeling a languid pleasure in joining the two halves of a bivalve, especially those lovely sunset shells that have rosy rays diverging from their crimson hinge over their polished surface, white, or just tinted with the hues of a daffodil sky. She never clasped a pair together without a little half-uttered ejaculation, " Oh, bring me and my dear young love thus together again!" And when she found a couple making a perfect heart, and holding together through all, she kissed it tenderly in the hope that thus it might be with her and with him whose hand and whose voice returned on her, calling her his dearest life!

She durst only quit the shells to eat the dinner which Madge served at one o'clock—a tolerable meal of slices of cold beef from a cook's-shop, but seasoned with sour looks and a murmur at ladies' fancies. The weariness and languor of the former day's exertions made her for the present disinclined to explore the house, even had she had time. and when twilight came there could have been little but fragments at the bottom of the case, though she could see no more to sort them.

And what were these noises around her making her start? Rats! Yes, here they were, venturing out from all the corners. They knew there had been food in the room. This was why Madge had those two gaunt, weird-looking cats in her kitchen! Aurelia went and sat on the step into the court to be out of their way, but Madge hunted her in that the door might be shut and barred; and when she returned trembling to the sitting-room, she heard such a scampering and a scrambling that she durst not enter, and betook herself to her chamber and to bed.

Alas! that was no refuge. She had been too much tired to hear anything the night before, but to-night there was scratching, nibbling, careering, fighting, squeaking, recoil and rally, charge and rout, as the grey Hanover rat fought his successful battle with his black English cousin all over the floors and stairs—nay, once or twice came rushing up and over the bed—frightening its occupant almost out of her senses, as she cowered under the bedclothes, not at all sure that they would not proceed to eating her. Happily daylight came early. Aurelia, at its first ray, darted across the room, starting in horror when she touched a soft thing with her bare foot, opened the shutter, and threw open the casement. Light drove the enemy back to their holes, and she had a few hours' sleep, but when Mrs. Loveday came to the room when she was nearly dressed, she exclaimed, " Why, miss, you look paler than you did yesterday."

" The rats ! " said Aurelia under her breath.

" Ah ! the rats ! Of course they are bad enough in an old desolate place like this. But you've done the shells right beautiful, that I will say ; and you may leave this house this very day if you will only give your consent to what my Lady asks. You shall be sent down this very day to Carminster, if so be you'll give up that ring of yours, and sign a paper giving up all claim to be married to his Honour See, here it is, all ready, in my Lady's letter."

" I cannot," said Aurelia, with her hands behind her.

"You can read my Lady's letter," said Loveday; "that can do you no harm."

Aurelia felt she must do that at least.

"CHILD,

"I will overlook your Transgression on the One Condition, that you sign this Paper and send it with your so-called Wedding Ring back to me immediately. Otherwise you must take the Consequences, and remain where you are till after my Son's Marriage.

"URANIA BELAMOUR."

The paper was a formal renunciation of all rights or claims from the fictitious marriage by which she had been deceived, and an absolute pledge never to renew any contract with Sir Amyas Belamour, Knight Baronet, who had grossly played on her.

"No, I cannot," said Aurelia, pushing it from her.

"Indeed, miss, I would not persuade you to it if it were not for your own good; but you may be sure it is no use holding out against her

Ladyship. If you sign it now, and give it up honourable, she will send Mr. Dove home with you, and there you'll be as if nothing had been amiss, no one knowing nothing about it; but if you persist it will not make the marriage a bit more true, and you will only be kept moped up in this dismal place till his Honour is married, and there's no saying what worse my Lady may do to you."

Another night of rats came up before Aurelia's imagination in contrast with the tender welcome at home; but the white face and the tones that had exclaimed, "Madam, what are you doing to my wife?" arose and forbade her. She would not fail him. So she said firmly once more, "No, Mrs. Loveday, I cannot. I do not know what lawyers may say, but I feel myself bound to Sir Amyas, and I will not break my vow—God helping me," she added under her breath.

"You must write it to her ladyship then. She will never take such a message through me. Here is paper and pen that I brought, in hopes that you would be wise and submit for your honoured father's sake."

"My father cannot be persecuted for what he has nothing to do with," said Aurelia, with the gentle dignity that had grown on her since her troubles. And taking the pen, she wrote her simple refusal, signing it Aurelia Belamour.

"As you please, ma'am," said Mrs. Loveday, "but I have my Lady's orders to bring this paper every day till you sign it, and it would be better for you if you would do it at once."

Aurelia only shook her head, and asked if Mrs. Loveday had seen that she had finished sorting the shells. Yes; and as she was now dressed they went down together to the sitting-room. The shutters were still closed, Madge would not put a hand to the room except on compulsion, and Aurelia's enemies had left evidence of their work; not only was the odour of the room like that of a barn, but the paper bags had in some cases been bitten through, and the shells scattered about, and of the loaf and butter which Aurelia had left on a high shelf in the cupboard nothing remained but a few fragments.

Loveday was very much shocked, all the more

when Aurelia quietly said she should not mind it so much if the rats would only stay down stairs, and not run over her in bed.

"Yet you will not sign the paper."

"I cannot," again said Aurelia.

"My stars, I never could abear rats! Why they fly at one's throat sometimes!"

"I hope God will take care of me," said Aurelia, in a trembling voice. "He did last night."

Loveday began a formal leave-taking curtsy, but presently turned back. "There now," she said, "I cannot do it, I couldn't sleep a wink for thinking of you among the rats! Look here, I shall send a porter to bring away those shells if you'll make up their bags again that the nasty vermin have eaten, and there's a little terrier dog about the place that no one will miss, he shall bring it down, and depend upon it, the rats won't venture near it."

"Oh! thank you, Mrs. Loveday, how good you are!"

"Ah, don't then! If you could say that my dear!"

Mrs. Loveday hurried away, and after breakfasting, Aurelia repaired the ravages of the rats, and made a last sorting of the residuum of shell dust, discovering numerous minute beauties, which awoke in her the happy thought of the Creator's individual love.

She had not yet finished before Madge's voice was heard in querulous anger, and a heavy tread came along with her. A big man, who could have carried ten times the weight of the box of shells, came in with a little white dog with black ears, under his arm.

"There," said the amiable guardian of the house, "that smart madam says that it's her ladyship's pleasure you should have that little beast to keep down the rats. As if my cats was not enough! But mind you, Madam Really, if so be he meddles with my cats, it will be the worse for him."

The porter took up the box, and departed, and Aurelia was left with her new companion sniffing all round the room, much excited by the neighbourhood of his natural enemies. However, he obeyed her call, and let her make friends, and read the name on the brass plate upon his collar. When she read " Sir A. Belamour, Bart.," she took the little dog in her arms and kissed its white head.

Being fairly rested, and having no task to accomplish, she felt the day much longer, though less solitary, in the companionship of the dog, to whom she whispered many fond compliments, and vain questions as to his name. With him at her heels, and Madge and her cats safely shut into the kitchen, she took courage to wander about the dull court, and then to explore the mansion and try to get a view from the higher windows, in case they were not shuttered up like the lower ones. The emptiness of Bowstead was nothing to this, and she smiled to herself at having thought herself a prisoner there.

Most of the rooms were completely dismantled, or had only ghastly rags of torn leather or tapestry hanging to their walls. The upper windows, however, were merely obscured by dust and cobwebs. Her own bedroom windows only showed the tall front of an opposite house, but climbing to the higher storey, she could see at the back over the garden wall the broad sheet of the Thames, covered with boats and wherries, and the banks provided with steps and stairs, at the opening of every street on the opposite side, where she beheld a confused mass of trees, churches, and houses Nearer, the view to the westward was closed in by a stately edifice which she did not know to be Somerset House; and from another window on the east side of the house she saw, over numerous tiled roofs, a gateway which she guessed to be Temple Bar, and a crowded thoroughfare, where the people looked like ants, toiling towards the great dome that rose in the misty distance. Was this the way she was to see London?

Coming down with a lagging step, she met Madge's face peering up. "Humph! there you be, my fine miss! No gaping after sweethearts from the window, or it will be the worse for you."

The terrier growled, as having already adopted his young lady's defence, and Aurelia, dreading a perilous explosion of his zeal in her cause, hurried him into her parlour.

CHAPTER XII.

THE SECOND TASK.

> Hope no more,
> Since thou art furnished with hidden lore,
> To 'scape thy due reward if any day
> Without some task accomplished pass away.
>
> MOORE.

THE little dog's presence was a comfort, but his night of combat and scuffling was not a restful one, and the poor prisoner's sickness of heart and nervous terrors grew upon her every hour, with misgivings lest she should be clinging to a shadow, and sacrificing her return to Betty's arms for a phantom. There were moments when her anguish of vague terror and utter loneliness impelled her to long to sign her renunciation that moment; and when she thought of recurring hours and weeks of such days and such nights her spirit quailed within her, and Loveday might have found her less calmly steadfast had she come in the morning.

She did not come, and this in itself was a disappointment, for at least she brought a human voice and a pitying countenance which, temptress though she might be, had helped to bear Aurelia through the first days. Oh! could she but find anything to do! She had dusted her two rooms as well as she could consistently with care for the dress she could not change. She blamed herself extremely for having forgotten her Bible and Prayer-book when hastily making up her bundle of necessaries, and though there was little chance that Madge should possess either, or be able to read, she nerved herself to ask. "Bible! what should ye want of a Bible, unless to play the hypocrite? I hain't got none!" was the reply.

So Aurelia could only walk up and down the court trying to repeat the Psalms, and afterwards the poetry she had learnt for Mr. Belamour's benefit, sometimes deriving comfort from the promises, but oftener wondering whether he had indeed deserted her in anger at her distrustful curiosity. She tried to scrape the mossgrown Triton, she crept up stairs to the window that looked towards the City, and cleared off some of the dimness, and she got a needle and thread and tried to darn the holes in the curtains and cushions, but the rotten stuff crumbled under her fingers, and would not hold the stitches. At last she found in a dusty corner a boardless book with neither beginning nor end, being Defoe's *Plague of London.* She read and read with a horrid fascination, believing every word of it, wondering whether this house could have been infected, and at length feeling for the plague spot!

A great church-clock enabled her to count the hours! Oh, how many there were of them! How many more would there be? This was only her second day, and deliverance could not come for weeks, were her young husband—if husband he were—ever so faithful. How should she find patience in this dreariness, interspersed with fits of alarm lest he should be dangerously ill and suffering? She fell on her knees and prayed for him and for herself!

Here it was getting dark again, and Madge would hunt her in presently and shut the shutters. Hark! what was that? A bell echoing over the house! Madge came after her. "Where are you, my fine mistress! Go you into your parlour, I say," and she turned the key upon the prisoner, whose heart beat like a bird fluttering in a cage. Suddenly her door was opened, and in darted Fidelia and Lettice, who flung themselves upon her with ecstatic shrieks of "Cousin Aura, dear cousin Aura!" Loveday was behind, directing the bringing in of trunks from a hackney coach. All she said was, "My Lady's daughters are to be with you for the night, madam; I must not say more, for her ladyship is waiting for me."

She was gone, while the three were still in the glad tangle of an embrace beginning again and again, with all sorts of little exclamations from the children, into which Aurelia broke with the inquiry for their brother. "He is much better," said Fay. "He is to get up to-morrow, and then he will come and find you."

"Have you seen him?"

"Oh, yes, and he says it is Sister Aura, and not Cousin Aura—"

"My dear, dear little sisters—" and she hugged them again.

"I was sitting upon his bed," said Letty, "and we were all talking about you when my Lady mamma came. Are mothers kinder than Lady mammas?"

"Was she angry?" asked Aurelia.

"Oh! she frightened me," said Fay. "She said we were pert, forward misses, and we must hold our tongues, for we should be whipped if we ever said your name, Cousin—Sister Aura, again; and she would not let us go to wish Brother Amyas good-bye this morning."

Aurelia's heart could not but leap with joy that her tyrant should have failed in carrying to Bowstead the renunciation of the marriage. Whether Lady Belamour meant it or not, she had made resistance much easier by the company of

Faith and Hope, if only for a single night. She gathered from their prattle that their mother, having found that their talk with their brother was all of the one object of his thoughts, had carried them off summarily, and had been since driving about London in search of a school at which to leave them; but they were too young for Queen's Square, and there was no room at another house at which Lady Belamour had applied. She would not take them home, being, of course, afraid of their tongues, and in her perplexity had been reduced to letting them share Aurelia's captivity at least for the night.

What joy it was! They said it was an ugly dark house, but Aurelia's presence was perfect content to them, and theirs was to her comparative felicity, assuring her as they did, through their childish talk, of Sir Amyas's unbroken love and of Mr. Belamour's endeavours to find her. What mattered it that Madge was more offended than ever, and refused to make the slightest exertion for "the Wayland brats at that time of night" without warning. They had enough for supper, and if Aurelia had not, their company was worth much more to her than a full meal. The terrier's rushes after rats were only diversion now, and when all three nestled together in the big bed, the fun was more delightful than ever. Between those soft caressing creatures Aurelia heard no rats, and could well bear some kicks at night, and being drummed awake at some strange hour in the morning.

Mrs. Loveday arrived soon after the little party had gone down stairs. She said the children were to remain until her ladyship had decided where to send them; and she confirmed their report that his Honour was recovering quickly. As soon as he was sufficiently well to leave Bowstead he was to be brought to London, and married to Lady Arabella before going abroad to make the grand tour; and as a true well-wisher, Mrs. Loveday begged Miss Delavie not to hold out when it was of no use, for her Ladyship declared that her contumacy would be the worse for her. Aurelia's garrison was, however, too well reinforced for any vague alarms to shake even her outworks, and she only smiled her refusal, as in truth Mrs. Loveday must have expected, for it appeared that she had secured a maid to attend on the prisoners; an extremely deaf woman, who only spoke in the broken imperfect mode of those who have never heard their own voice, deficiencies that made it possible that Madge would keep the peace with her.

Lady Belamour had also found another piece of work for Aurelia. A dark cupboard was opened, revealing shelves piled with bundles of old letters and papers. There was a family tradition that one of the ladies of the Delavie family had been an attendant of Mary of Scotland for a short time, and had received from her a recipe for preserving the complexion and texture of the skin, devised by the French Court perfumer. Nobody had ever seen this precious prescription; but it was presumed to be in the archives of the family, and her ladyship sent word that if Miss Delavie wished to deserve her favour she would put her French to some account and discover it.

A severe undertaking it was. Piles of yellow letters, files of dusty accounts, multitudes of receipts, more than one old will had to be conned before it was possible to be certain they were not the nostrum. In the utter solitude, even this occupation would have been valuable, but with the little girls about her, and her own and their personal property, she had alternative employments enough to make it an effort to apply herself to this.

Why should she? she asked herself more than once; but then came the recollection that if she showed herself willing to obey and gratify my Lady, it might gain her good will, and if Sir Amyas should indeed hold out till Mr. Wayland came home —Her heart beat wildly at the vision of hope.

She worked principally at the letters, after the children had gone to bed, taking a packet up stairs with her, and sitting in the bedroom, deciphering them as best she might by the light of the candles that Loveday had brought her.

Every morning Loveday appeared with supplies, and messages from her Ladyship, that it was time Miss submitted; but she was not at all substantially unkind, and showed increasing interest in her captive, though always impressing on her that her obstinacy was all in vain. My Lady was angered enough at his Honour having got up from his sick bed and gone off to Carminster, and if Miss did not wish to bring her father into trouble she must yield. No, this gladdened rather than startled Aurelia, though her heart sank within her when she was warned that Mr. Wayland had been taken by the corsairs, so that my Lady would have the ball at her own foot now. The term of waiting seemed indefinitely prolonged.

The confinement to the dingy house and courtyard was trying to all the three, who had been used to run about in the green park and breezy fields; but Aurelia did her best to keep her little companions happy and busy, and the sense of the insecurity of her tenure of their company aided her the more to meet with good temper and sweetness the various rubs incidental to their captivity in this close warm house in the hottest of summer weather. The pang she had felt at her own fretfulness, when she thought she had lost them, made her guard the more against giving way to impatience if they were troublesome or hard to please. Indeed, she was much more gentle and equable now, in the strength of her resolution, than she had been when uplifted by her position, yet doubtful of its mysteries.

Sundays were the most trying time. The lack of occupation in the small space was wearisome, and Aurelia's heart often echoed the old strains of Tate and Brady,

> I sigh whene'er my musing thoughts
> Those happy days present,
> When I with troops of pious friends
> Thy temple did frequent.

She and her charges climbed up to the window above, which happily had a broken pane, tried to identify the chimes of the church bells by the notable nursery rhyme,

> Oranges and lemons,
> Say the bells of St. Clements, &c.,

watched the church-goers as far as they could see them, and then came down to such reading of the service and other Sunday occupations as Aurelia could devise. On the second Sunday of her durance it was such a broiling day that, unable to bear the heat of her parlour, she established herself and her charges in a nook of the court, close under the window, but shaded by the wall, which was covered with an immense bush of overhanging ivy, and by the elm tree in the court. Here she made Fay and Letty say their catechism, and the Psalm she had been teaching them in the week, and then rewarded them with a Bible story, that of Daniel in the den of lions. Once or twice the terrier (whose name she had learnt was Bob) had pricked his ears, and the children had thought there was a noise, but the sparrows in the ivy might be accountable for a great deal, and the little ones were too much wrapped in her tale to be attentive to anything else.

"Then it came true!" said Letty. "His God Whom he trusted did deliver him out of the den of lions?"

"God always does deliver people when they trust Him," said Fay, with gleaming eyes.

"Yes, one way or the other," said Aurelia.

"How do you think He will deliver us?" asked Letty; "for I am sure this is a den, though there are no lions."

"I do not know how," said Aurelia, "but I know He will bear us through it, as long as we trust Him and do nothing wrong," and she looked up at the bright sky with hope and strength in her face.

"Hark! what's that?" cried Letty, and Bob leapt up and barked as a great sob became plainly audible, and within the room appeared Mrs. Loveday, her face all over tears, which she was fast wiping away as she rose up from crouching with her head against the window-sill.

"I beg your pardon, ma'am," said she, her voice still broken when she rejoined them, "but I would not interrupt you, so I waited within; and oh, it was so like my poor old mother at home, it quite overcame me! I did not think there was anything so near the angels left on earth."

"Nay, Loveday," said Fay, apprehending the words in a different sense, "the angels are just as near us as ever they were to Daniel, only we cannot see them. Are they not, Cousin Aura?"

"Indeed they are, and we may be as sure that they will shut the lions' mouths," said Aurelia.

"Ah! may they," sighed Loveday, who had by this time mastered her agitation, and remembered that she must discharge herself of her messages, and return hastily to my Lady's toilette.

"I have found the recipe," said Aurelia. " Here it is." And she put into Loveday's hand a yellow letter, bearing the title in scribbled writing, "*Poure Embellire et blanchire la Pel, de part de Maistre Raoul, Parfumeur de la Royne Catherine.*"

CHAPTER XIII.

LIONS.

> The helmet then of darkness Pallas donned,
> To hide her presence from the sight of man.
> *Derby's* HOMER.

THE next morning Loveday returned with orders from Lady Belamour that Miss Delavie should translate the French recipe, and make a fair copy of it. It was not an easy task, for the MS. was difficult and the French old; whereas Aurelia lived on the modern side of the *Academie*, and her French was that of Fénélon and Racine.

However, she went to work as best she could in her cool corner, guessing at many of the words by lights derived from *Comenius*, and had just made out that the chief ingredients were pounded pearls and rubies, mixed with white of eggs laid by pullets under a year old, during the waxing of the April moon, when she heard voices chattering in the hall, and a girlish figure appeared in a light cloak and calash, whom Loveday seemed to be guiding, and yet keeping as much repressed as she could.

"Gracious Heavens!" were the first words to be distinguished; "what a frightful old place; enough to make one die of the dismals! I won't live here when I'm married, I promise Sir Amyas! Bless me, is this the wench?"

"Your Ladyship promised to be careful," entreated Loveday, while Aurelia rose, with a graceful gesture of acknowledgment, which, however, remained unnoticed, the lady apparently considering herself unseen.

"Who are these little girls?" asked she, in a giggling whisper. "Little Waylands? Then it is true," she cried, with a peal of shrill laughter. "There are three of them, only Lady Belamour shuts them up here because she can't drown them like kittens—I wonder she did not. Oh, what sport! Won't I tease her now that I know her secret!"

"Your ladyship!" intreated Loveday in distress in an audible aside, "you will undo me." Then coming forward, she said, "You did not expect me at this hour, madam; but if your French copy be finished, my Lady would like to have it at once."

"I have written it out once as well as I could," said Aurelia, "but I have not translated it; I will find the copy."

She rose and found the stranger full before her in the doorway, gazing at her with an enormous pair of sloe-black eyes, under heavy inky brows, set in a hard, red-complexioned face. She burst into a loud, hoydenish laugh as Loveday tried to stammer something about a friend of her own.

"Never mind, the murder's out, good Mrs. Abigail," she cried, "it is me. I was determined to see the wench that has made such a fool of young Belamour. I vow I can't guess what he means by it. Why, you are a poor pale tallow-candle, without a bit of colour in your face. Look at me! Shall you ever have such a complexion as mine, with ever so much rouge?"

"I think not," said Aurelia, with one look at the peony face.

"Do you know who I am, miss? I am the Lady Bella Mar. The Countess of Aresfield is my mamma. I shall have Battlefield when she dies, and twenty thousand pounds on my wedding-day. The Earl of Aresfield and Colonel Mar are my brothers, and a wretched little country girl like you is not to come between me and what my mamma has fixed for me; so you must give it up at once, for you see he belongs to me."

"Not yet, madam," said Aurelia.

"What do you say? Do you pretend that your masquerade was worth a button?"

"That is not my part to decide," said Aurelia. "I am bound by it, and have no power to break it."

"You mean the lawyers! Bless you, they will never give it to you against me! You'd best give it up at once, and if you want a husband, my mamma has one ready for you."

"I thank her ladyship," said Aurelia, with simple dignity, "but I will not give her the trouble."

She glanced at her wedding ring, and so did Lady Belle, who screamed, "You've the impudence to wear that! Give it to me."

"I cannot," repeated Aurelia.

"You cannot, you insolent, vulgar, low"—

"Hush! hush, my lady," entreated Loveday. "Come away, I beg of your ladyship!"

"Not till I have made that impudent hussy give me that ring," cried Belle, stamping violently. "What's that you say?"

"That your ladyship asks what is impossible," said Aurelia, firmly.

"Take that then, insolent minx!" cried the girl, flying forward and violently slapping Aurelia's soft cheeks, and making a snatch at her hair.

Loveday screamed, Letty cried, but Fidelia and Bob both rushed forward to Aurelia's defence, one with her little fists clenched, beating Lady Belle back, the other tearing at her skirts with his teeth. At that moment a man's step was heard, and a tall, powerful officer was among them, uttering a fierce imprecation. "You little vixen, at your tricks again," he said, taking Belle by the waist, while she kicked and screamed in vain. She was like an angry cat in his arms. "Be quiet, Belle," he said, backing into the sitting-room. "Let Loveday compose your dress. Recover your senses, and I shall take you home: I wish it was to the whipping you deserve."

He thrust her in, waved aside Loveday's excuses about her ladyship not being denied, and stood with his back to the door as she bounced shrieking against it from within.

"I fear this little devil has hurt you, madam," he said.

"Not at all, I thank you, sir," said Aurelia, though one side of her face still tingled.

"She made at you like a little game-cock," he said. "I am glad I was in time. I followed when I found she had slipped away from Lady Belamour's, knowing that her curiosity is only equalled by her spite. By Jove, it is well that her nails did not touch that angel face!"

Aurelia could only curtsey and thank him, hoping within herself that Lady Belle would soon recover, and wondering how he had let himself in.

There was something in his manner of examining her with his eyes that made her supremely uncomfortable. He uttered fashionable expletives of admiration under his breath, and she turned aside in displeasure, bending down to Fidelia. He went on, "You must be devilishly moped in this dungeon of a place! Cannot we contrive something better?"

"Thank you, sir, I have no complaint to make. Permit me to see whether the Lady Arabella is better."

"I advise you not. Those orbs are too soft and sparkling to be exposed to her talons. 'Pon my honour, I pity young Belamour. But there is no help for it, and such charms ought not to be wasted in solitude on his account. These young lads are as fickle as the weather-cock, and have half-a-dozen fancies in as many weeks. Come now, make me your friend, and we will hit on some device for delivering the enchanted princess from her durance vile."

"Thank you, sir, I promised Lady Belamour to make no attempt to escape."

At that moment out burst Lady Belle, shouting with laughter: "Ho! ho! Have I caught you, brother, gallanting away with Miss? What will my lady say? Pretty doings!"

She had no time for more. Her brother fiercely laid hold of her, and bore her away with a peremptory violence that she could not resist, and only turning at the hall door to make one magnificent bow.

Loveday was obliged to follow, and the children were left clinging to Aurelia and declaring that the dreadful young lady was as bad as the lions; while Aurelia, glowing with shame and resentment at what she felt as insults, had a misgiving that her protector had been the worse lion of the two.

She had no explanation of the invasion till the next morning, when Loveday appeared full of excuses and apologies. From the fact of Lady Aresfield's carriage having been used on Aurelia's arrival, her imprisonment was known, and Lady Belle, spending a holiday at Lady Belamour's, had besieged Loveday with entreaties to take her to see her rival. As the waiting-woman said, for fear of the young lady's violent temper, but more probably in consideration of her bribes, she had yielded, hoping that Lady Belle would be satisfied with a view from the window, herself unseen. However, from that moment all had been taken out of the hands of Loveday, and she verily believed the Colonel had made following his sister an excuse for catching a sight of Miss Delavie, for he had been monstrously smitten even with the glimpse he had had of her in the carriage. And now, as his sister had cut short what he had to say, he had written her a billet. And Loveday held out a perfumed letter.

Aurelia's eyes flashed, and she drew herself up: "You forget, Loveday, I promised to receive no letters!"

"Bless me, ma'am, they, that are treated as my lady treats you, are not bound to be so particular as that."

"O fie, Loveday," said Aurelia earnestly, "you have been so kind, that I thought you would be faithful. This is not being faithful to your lady, nor to me."

"It is only from my wish to serve you, ma'am," said Loveday in her fawning voice. "How can I bear to see a beautiful young lady like you, that ought to be the star of all the court, mewed up here for the sake of a young giddy pate like his Honour, when there's one of the first gentlemen in the land ready to be at your feet?"

"For shame! for shame!" exclaimed Aurelia, crimson already. "You know I am married."

"And you will not take the letter, nor see what the poor gentleman means? May be he wants to reconcile you with my lady, and he has power with her."

Aurelia took the letter, and, strong paper though it was, tore it across and across till it was all in fragments, no bigger than daisy flowers. "There," she said, "you may tell him what I have done to his letter."

Loveday stared for a minute, then exclaimed, "You are in the right, my dear lady. Oh, I am a wretch—a wretch—" and she went away sobbing.

Aurelia hoped the matter was ended. It had

given her a terrible feeling of insecurity, but she found to her relief that Madge was really more trustworthy than Loveday. She overheard from the court a conversation at the back door in which Madge was strenuously refusing admission to some one who was both threatening and bribing her, all in vain; but she was only beginning to breathe freely when Loveday brought, not another letter, but what was less easy to stop, a personal message from "that poor gentleman."

"Loveday, after what you said yesterday, how can you be so—wicked?" said Aurelia.

"Indeed, miss, 'tis only as your true well-wisher."

Aurelia turned away to leave the room.

"Yes, it is, ma'am! On my bended knees I will swear it," cried Loveday, throwing herself on them and catching her dress. "It is because I know my lady has worse in store for you!"

"Nothing can be worse than wrong-doing," said Aurelia.

"Ah! you don't know. Now, listen, one moment. I would not—indeed I would not—if I did not know that he meant true and honourable—as he does, indeed he does. He is madder after you than ever he was for my lady, for he says you have all her beauty. and freshness and simplicity besides. He is raving. And you should never leave me, indeed you should not, miss, if you slipped out after me in Deb's muffler—and we'd go to the Fleet. I have got a cousin there, poor fellow—he is always in trouble, but he is a real true parson notwithstanding, and I'd never leave your side till the knot was tied fast. Then you would laugh at my lady, and be one of the first ladies in the land, for my Lord Aresfield is half a fool, and can't live long, and when you are a countess you will remember your poor Loveday."

"Let me go. You have said too much to a married woman," said Aurelia, and as the maid began the old demonstrations of the invalidity of the marriage, and the folly of adhering to it when nobody knew where his honour was gone, she said resolutely, "I shall write to Lady Belamour to send me a more trustworthy messenger."

On this Loveday fairly fell on the floor, grovelling

in her wild entreaty that my Lady might hear nothing of this, declaring that it was not so much for the sake of the consequences to herself as to the young lady, for there was no guessing what my lady might not be capable of if she guessed at Colonel Mar's admiration of her prisoner. Aurelia, frightened at her violence, finally promised not to appeal to her ladyship as long as Loveday abstained from transmitting his messages, but on the least attempt on her part to refer to him, a complaint should certainly be made to my lady.

"Very well, madam," said Loveday, wiping her eyes. "I only hope it will not be the worse for you in the end, and that you will not wish you had listened to poor Loveday's advice."

"I can never wish to have done what I know to be a great sin," said Aurelia, gravely.

"Ah! you little know!" said Loveday, shaking her head sadly and ominously.

Something brought to Aurelia's lips what she had been teaching the children last Sunday, and she answered,

"My God, in Whom I have trusted, is able to

deliver me out of the mouth of the lions, and He will deliver me out of thy hand."

"Oh! if ever there were one whom He should deliver!" broke out Loveday, and again she went away weeping bitterly.

Aurelia could not guess what the danger the woman threatened could be; so many had been mentioned as possible. A forcible marriage, incarceration in some lonely country place, a vague threat of being taken beyond seas to the plantations—all these had been mentioned; but she was far more afraid of Colonel Mar forcing his way in and carrying her off, and this kept her constantly in a state of nervous watchfulness, always listening by day and hardly able to sleep by night.

Once she had a terrible alarm, on a Sunday. Letty came rushing to her, declaring that Jumbo, dear Jumbo, and a gentleman were in the front court. Was it really Jumbo? Oh, yes, it was a black man. Come and see! No, she durst not, and Fay almost instantly declared that Madge had shut them out. The children both insisted that Jumbo it was, but Aurelia would not believe that it could be anything but an attempt of her enemies. She interrogated Madge, who had grown into a certain liking for one so submissive and inoffensive. Madge shook her head, could not guess how such folks had got into the court, was sure they were after no good, and declared that my Lady should hear of all the strange doings, and the letters that had been left with her. Oh, no, she knew better than to give them, but my Lady should see them.

CHAPTER XIV.

THE COSMETIC.

> But one more task I charge thee with to-day,
> For unto Proserpine then take thy way,
> And give this golden casket to her hands.
>
> MORRIS.

LATE on that Sunday afternoon, a muffled and masked figure came through the house into the court behind, and after the first shock Aurelia was relieved to see that it was too tall, and moved too gracefully, to belong to Loveday.

"Why, child, what a colour you have!" said Lady Belamour, taking off her mask. "You need no aids to nature at your happy age. That is right, children," as they curtsied and kissed her hand. "Go into the house, I wish to speak with your cousin."

Lady Belamour's unfailing self-command gave her such dignity that she seemed truly a grand and majestic dame dispensing justice, and the gentle, shrinking Aurelia like a culprit on trial before her.

"You have been here a month, Aurelia Delavie. Have you come to your senses, and are you ready to sign this paper?"

"No, madam, I cannot."

"Silly fly; you are as bent as ever on remaining in the web in which a madman and a foolish boy have involved you?"

"I cannot help it, madam."

"Oh! I thought," and her voice became harshly clear, though so low, "that you might have other schemes, and be spreading your toils at higher game."

"Certainly not, madam."

"Your colour shows that you understand, in spite of all your pretences."

"I have never used any pretences, my lady," said Aurelia, looking up in her face with clear innocent eyes.

"You have had no visitors? None!"

"None, madam, except once when the Lady Arabella Mar forced her way in, out of curiosity, I believe, and her brother followed to take her away."

"Her brother? You saw him?" Each word came out edged like a knife from between her nearly closed lips.

"Yes, madam."

"How often?"

"That once."

"That has not hindered a traffic in letters."

"Not on my side, madam. I tore to fragments unread the only one I received. He had no right to send it!"

"Certainly not. You judge discreetly, Miss Delavie. In fact you are too transcendent a paragon to be retained here." Then, biting her lip, as if the bitter phrase had escaped unawares, she smiled blandly and said, "My good girl, you have merited to be returned to your friends. You may pack your mails and those of the children!"

Aurelia shuddered with gladness, but Lady

Belamour checked her thanks by continuing, "One service you must first do for me. My perfumer is at a loss to understand your translation of the recipe for Queen Mary's wash. I wish you to read and explain it to her."

"Certainly, madam."

"She lives near Greenwich Park," continued Lady Belamour, "and as I would not have the secret get abroad, I shall send a wherry to take you to the place early to-morrow morning. Can you be ready by eight o'clock?"

Aurelia readily promised, her heart bounding at the notion of a voyage down the river after her long imprisonment and at the promise of liberty! She thought her husband must still be true to her, since my lady would have been the first to inform her of his defection, and as long as she had her ring and her certificate, she could feel little doubt that her father would be able to establish her claims. And oh! to be with him and Betty once more!

She was ready in good time, and had spent her leisure in packing. When Loveday appeared, she was greeted with a petition that the two little girls might accompany her; but this was refused at once, and the waiting-maid added in her caressing, consoling tone that Mrs. Dove was coming with their little brother and sister to take them a drive into the country. They skipped about with glee, following Aurelia to the door of the court, and promising her posies of honeysuckles and roses, and she left her dear love with them for Amoret and Nurse Dove.

At the door was a sedan chair, in which Aurelia was carried to some broad stone stairs, beside which lay a smartly-painted, trim-looking boat with four stout oarsmen. She was handed into the stern, Loveday sitting opposite to her. The woman was unusually silent, and could hardly be roused to reply to Aurelia's eager questions as she passed the gardens of Lincoln's Inn, saw St Paul's rise above her, shot beneath the arch of London Bridge, and beheld the massive walls of the Tower with its low-browed arches opening above their steps. Whenever a scarlet uniform came in view, how the girl's eyes strained after it, thinking of one impossible, improbable chance of a recognition! Once or twice she thought of a far more terrible chance, and wondered whether Lady Belamour knew how little confidence could be placed in Loveday; but she was sure that their expedition was my lady's own device, and the fresh air and motion, with all the new scenes, were so delightful to her that she could not dwell on any alarms.

On, on, Redriffe, as the watermen named Rotherhithe, was on one bank, the marshes of the Isle of Dogs were gay with white cotton-grass and red rattle on the other. Then came the wharves and building yards of Deptford, and beyond them rose the trees of Greenwich Park, while the river below exhibited a forest of masts. The boat stopped at a landing-place to a little garden, with a sanded path, between herbs and flowers. "This is Mistress Darke's" said Loveday, and as a little dwarfish lad came to the gate, she said, "We would speak with your mistress."

"On your own part?"

"From the great lady in Hanover Square."

The lad came down to assist in their landing,

and took them up the path to a little cupboard of a room, scented with a compound of every imaginable perfume. Bottles of every sort of essence, pomade, and cosmetic were ranged on shelves, or within glass doors, interspersed with masks, boxes for patches, bunches of false hair, powder puffs, curling-irons, and rare feathers. An alembic was in the fireplace, and pen and ink, in a strangely-shaped standish, were on the table. Altogether there was something uncanny about the look and air of the room which made Aurelia tremble, especially as she perceived that Loveday was both frightened and distressed.

The mistress of the establishment speedily appeared. She had been a splendid Jewish beauty, and still in middle age, had great owl-like eyes. and a complexion that did credit to her arts ; but there was something indescribably repulsive in her fawning, deferential curtsey, as she said, in a flattering tone, with a slightly foreign accent, " The pretty lady is come, as our noble dame promised, to explain to the poor Cora Darke the great queen's secret ! Ah! how good it is to have learning. The lovely young lady has them both, the beauty and the learning. What would not my clients give for such a skin as hers! And I have many more, and greater than you would think, come to the poor Cora's cottage. There was a countess here but yesterday to ask how to blanch the complexion of miladi her daughter, who is about to wed a young baronet, beautiful as Love. Bah! I might as well try to whiten a clove gillyflower! Yet what has not nature done for this lovely miss?"

"Shall I read you the paper?" said Aurelia, longing to end this part of the affair.

"Be seated, fair and gracious lady."

Aurelia tried to wave aside a chair, but Mrs. Darke, on the plea of looking over the words as she read, got her down upon a low couch, putting her own stout person and hooked face in unpleasant proximity, while she asked questions, and Aurelia mentioned her own conjectures on the obsolete French of the recipe, while she perceived, to her alarm, that the woman understood the technical terms much better than she did, and that her ignorance could have been only an excuse.

At last it was finished, and she rose, saying it was time to return to the boat.

"Nay, madam, that cannot be yet," said Loveday; "the watermen are gone to rest and dine, and we must wait for the tide to shoot the bridge."

"Then pray let us go out and walk in Greenwich Park," exclaimed Aurelia, longing to escape from this den.

"The sweet young lady will take something in the meantime?" said Mrs. Darke.

"I thank you, I have breakfasted," said Aurelia.

"My Lady intended us to eat here," said Loveday in an undertone to her young lady, as their hostess bustled out. "She will make it good to Mrs. Darke."

"I had rather go to the inn—I have money—or sit in the park," she added as Loveday looked as if going to the inn were an improper proposal. "Could we not buy a loaf and eat in the park? I should like it so much better."

"One cup of coffee," said Mrs. Darke, entering; "the excellent Mocha that I get from the Turkey captains."

She set down on a small table a wonderful cup of Eastern porcelain, and some little sugared cakes, and Aurelia, not to be utterly ungracious, tasted one, and began on the coffee, which was so hot that it had to be taken slowly. As she sipped a soothing drowsiness came over her, which at first was accounted for by the warm room after her fresh row on the river; but it gained upon her, and instead of setting out for her walk she fell sound asleep in the corner of the couch.

"It has worked. It is well," said Mrs. Darke, lifting the girl's feet on the couch, and producing a large pair of scissors.

Loveday could not repress a little shriek.

"Hush!" as the woman untied the black silk hood, drew it gently off, and then undid the ribbon that confined the victim's abundant tresses. "Bah! it will be grown by the time she arrives, and if not so long as at present, what will they know of it? It will be the more agreeable surprise! Here, put yonder cloth under her head while I hold it up."

"I cannot," sobbed Loveday. "This is too much.

I never would have entered my Lady's service if I had known I was to be set to such as this."

"Come, come, Grace Loveday, I know too much of you for you to come the Precisian over me."

"Such a sweet innocent! So tender-hearted and civil too."

"Bless you, woman, you don't know what's good for her! She will be a very queen over the black slaves in the Indies. Captain Karen will tell you how the wenches thank him for having brought 'em out. They could never do any good here, you know, poor lasses; but out there, where white women are scarce, they are ready to worship the very ground they tread upon."

"I tell you she ain't one of that sort. She is a young lady of birth, a cousin of my Lady's own, as innocent as a babe, and there are two gentlemen, if not three, a dying for her."

"I lay you anything not one of 'em is worth old Mr. Van Draagen, who turns his thousands every month. 'Send me out a lady lass,' says he, 'one that will do me credit with the governor's lady.' Why she will have an estate as big as from here to Dover, and slaves to wait on her, so as she need never stoop to pick up her glove. He has been married twice before, and his last used to send orders for the best brocades in London. He stuck at no expense. The Queen has not finer gowns!"

"But to think of the poor child's waking up out at sea."

"Oh! Mrs. Karen will let her know she may think herself well off. I never let 'em go unless there's a married woman aboard to take charge of them, and that's why I kept your lady waiting till the *Red Cloud* was ready to sail. You may tell her Ladyship she could not have a better berth, and she'll want for nothing. I know what is due to the real quality, and I've put aboard all the toilette, and linen, and dresses as was bespoke for the last Mrs. Van Draagen, and there's a civil spoken wench aboard, that will wait on her for a consideration."

"Nay, but mistress," said Loveday, whispering: "I know those that would give more than you will ever get from my Lady if they found her safe here."

"Of course there are, or she would not be here now," said Mrs. Darke, with a horrid grin; "but than won't do, my lass. A lady that's afraid of exposure will pay you, if she pawns her last diamond, but a gentleman—why, he gets sick of his fancy, and snaps his fingers at them that helped him!" Then, looking keenly at Loveday, "You've not been playing me false, eh?"

"O no, no," hastily exclaimed Loveday, cowering at the malignant look.

"If so be you have, Grace Loveday, two can play at that game," said Mrs. Darke composedly. "There, I have left her enough to turn back. What hair it is! Feel the weight of it! There's not another head of that mouse-colour to match your Lady's in the kingdom," she added, smoothing out the severed tresses with the satisfaction of a connoisseur. "No wonder madame could not let this be wasted on the plantations, when you and I and M. le Friseur know her own hair is getting thinner than she would wish a certain Colonel to guess. There! the pretty dear, what a baby she looks! I will tie her on a cowl, lest she should take cold on the river. See these rings. Did your Lady give no charge about them?"

"I had forgot!" said the waiting-woman, confused; "she charged me to bring them back, old family jewels, she said, that must not be carried off to foreign parts; but I cannot, cannot do it. To rob that pretty creature in her sleep."

"Never fear. She'll soon have a store much finer than these! You fool, I tell you she will not wake these six or eight hours. Afraid? There, I'll do it! Ho! A ruby? A love-token, I wager; and what's this? A carved Cupid. I could turn a pretty penny by that, when your lady finds it convenient, and her luck at play goes against her. Eh! is this a wedding-ring? Best take that off; Mr. Van Draagen might not understand it, you see. Here they are. Have you a patch-box handy for them in your pocket? Why what ails the woman? You may thank your stars there's some one here with her wits about her! None of your whimpering, I say, here comes Captain Karen."

Two seafaring men here came up the garden

path, the foremost small and dapper, with a ready address and astute countenance. "All right, Mother Darkness, is our consignment ready? Aye, aye! And the freight?"

"This lady has it," said Mrs. Darke, pointing to Loveday; "I have been telling her she need have no fears for her young kinswoman in your hands, Captain."

He swore a round oath to that effect, and looking at the sleeping maiden, again swore that she was the choicest piece of goods ever confided to him, and that he knew better than let such an article arrive damaged. Mr. Van Draagen ought to come down handsomely for such an extra fine sample; but in the meantime he accepted the rouleau of guineas that Loveday handed to him, the proceeds, as she told Mrs. Darke, of my Lady's winnings last night at loo.

All was ready. Poor Aurelia was swathed from head to foot in a large mantle, like the chrysalis whose name she bore, the two sailors took her up between them, carried her to their boat, and laid her along in the stern. Then they pushed off and rowed down the river. Loveday looked up and looked down, then sank on the steps, convulsed with grief, sobbing bitterly. "She said He could deliver her from the mouth of the lions! And He has not," she murmured under her breath, in utter misery and hopelessness.

CHAPTER XV.

DOWN THE RIVER.

> The lioness, ye may move her
> To give o'er her prey,
> But ye'll ne'er stop a lover,
> He will find out the way.

ELIZABETH DELAVIE and her little brother were standing in the bay window of their hotel, gazing eagerly along the street in hopes of seeing the Major return, when Sir Amyas was seen riding hastily up on his charger, in full accoutrements, with a soldier following. In another moment he had dashed up stairs, and saying, "Sister, read that!" put into Betty's hand a slip of paper on which was written in pencil—

"If Sir A. B. would not have his true love kidnapped to the plantations, he had best keep watch on the river gate of Mistress Darke's garden at Greenwich. No time to lose."

"Who brought you this?" demanded Betty, as well as she could speak for horror.

"My mother's little negro boy, Syphax. He says Mrs. Loveday, her waiting-woman, gave it to him privately on the stairs, as she was about to get into a sedan, telling him I would give him a crown if he gave it me as I came off parade."

"Noon! Is there time?"

"Barely, but there shall be time. There is no time to seek your father."

"No, but I must come with you."

"The water is the quickest way. There are stairs near. I'll send my fellow to secure a boat."

"I will be ready instantly, while you tell your uncle. It might be better if he came."

Sir Amyas flew to his uncle's door, but found him gone out, and, in too great haste to inquire further, came down again to find Betty in cloak and hood. He gave her his arm, and, Eugene trotting after them, they hurried to the nearest stairs, remembering in dire confirmation what Betty had heard from the school-girl. Both had heard reports that young women were sometimes thus deported to become wives to the planters in the southern colonies or the West Indies, but that such a destiny should be intended for their own Aurelia, and by Lady Belamour, was scarcely credible. Doubts rushed over Betty, but she remembered what the school-girl had said of the captive being sent beyond seas; and at any rate, she must risk the expedition being futile when such issues hung upon it. And if they failed to meet her father, she felt that her presence might prevail when the undefined rights of so mere a lad as her companion might be disregarded.

His soldier servant had secured a boat, and they rapidly descended the river; Sir Amyas silent between suspense, dismay and shame for his mother, and Betty trying to keep Eugene quiet by hurried answers to his eager questions about all he saw. They had to get out at London Bridge, and take a fresh boat on the other side, a much larger one, with two oarsmen, and a grizzled old coxswain, with a pleasant honest countenance, who presently relieved Betty of all necessity of attending to, or answering, Eugene's chatter.

"Do you know where this garden is?" said she, leaning across to Sir Amyas, who had engaged the boat to go to Greenwich.

He started as if it were a new and sudden thought, and turning to the steersman demanded whether he knew Mrs. Darke's garden.

The old man gave a kind of grunt, and eyed the trio interrogatively, the young officer with his fresh, innocent, boyish face and brilliant undisguised uniform, the handsome child, the lady neither young, gay, nor beautiful, but unmistakeably a decorous gentlewoman.

"Do you know Mrs. Darke's?" repeated Sir Amyas.

"Aye, do I? Mayhap I know more about the place than you do."

There was that about his face that moved Betty and the young man to look at one another, and the former said, "She has had to do with—evil doings?"

"You may say that, ma'am."

"Then," they cried in one breath, "you will help us!" And in a very few words Betty explained their fears for her young sister, and asked whether he thought the warning possible.

"I've heard tell of such things!" said the old man between his teeth, "and Mother Darkness is one to do 'em. Help you to bring back the poor young lass? That we will, if we have to break down the door with our fists. And who is this young spark? Her brother or her sweetheart?"

"Her husband!" said Sir Amyas. "Her husband, from whom she has been cruelly spirited away. Aid me to bring her back, my good fellow, and nothing would be too much to reward you."

"Aye, aye, captain, Jem Green's not the man to see an English girl handed over to they slave-driving, outlandish chaps. But I say, I wish you'd got a cloak or summat to put over that scarlet and gold of yourn. It's a regular flag to put the old witch on her guard."

On that summer's day, however, no cloak was at hand. They went down the river very rapidly, for the tide was running out, and at length Jem Green pointed out the neat little garden. On the step sat a woman, apparently weeping bitterly.

Could it be the object of their search? No, but as they came nearer, and she was roused so as to catch sight of the scarlet coat, she beckoned and gesticulated with all her might; and as they approached Sir Amyas recognised her as his mother's maid.

"You will be in time yet," she cried breathlessly. "Oh! take me in, or you won't know the ship!"

So eager and terrified was she, that but for the old steersman's peremptory steadiness, her own life and theirs would have been in much peril, but she was safely seated at last, gasping out, "The *Red Cloud*, Captain Karen. They've been gone these ten minutes."

"Aye, aye," gruffly responded Green, and the oars moved rapidly, while Loveday with another sob cried, "Oh! sir, I thought you would never come!"

"You sent the warning?"

"Yes, sir, I knew nothing till the morning, when my Lady called me up. I lie in her room, you know. She had given all her orders, and I was to take the sweet lady and go down the river with her to Mrs. Darke, the perfuming woman my Lady has dealings with about her hair and complexion. There I was to stay with her till— till this same sea-captain was to come and carry her off where she would give no more trouble. Oh, sir, it was too much—and my Lady knew it, for she had tied my hands so that I had but a moment to scribble down that scrip, and bid Syphax take it to you. The dear lady! she said 'her God could deliver her out of the mouth of the lion,' and I could not believe it! I thought it too late!"

"How can we thank you," began Betty; but she was choked by intense anxiety, and Jem Green broke in with an inquiry where the ship was bound for. Loveday only had a general impression of the West Indies, and believed that the poor lady's destined spouse was a tobacconist, and as the boat was soon among a forest of shipping where it could not proceed so fast, Green had to inquire of neighbouring mariners where the *Red Cloud* was lying.

"The *Red Cloud*, Karen, weighs anchor for

Carolina at flood tide to-night. Skipper just going aboard," they were told.

Their speed had been so rapid that they were in time to see the boat alongside, and preparations being made to draw up some one or something on board. "Oh! that is she!" cried Loveday in great agitation. "They've drugged her. No harm done. She don't know it. But it is she!"

Sir Amyas, with a voice of thunder, called out "Halt, villain," at the same moment as Green shouted "Avast there, mate!" And their boat came dashing up alongside.

"Yield me up that lady instantly, fellow!" cried Sir Amyas, with his sword half drawn.

"And who are you, I should like to know," returned Karen, coolly, "swaggering at an honest man taking his freight and passengers aboard?"

"I'll soon show you!"

"Hush, sir," said Green, who had caught sight of pistols and cutlasses, "let me speak a moment. Look you here, skipper, this young gentleman and lady have right on their side. This is her sister, and he is her husband. They are people of condition, as you see."

"All's one to me on the broad seas."

"That may be," said Green, "but you see you can't weigh anchor these three hours or more; and what's to hinder the young captain here from swearing against you before a magistrate, and getting your vessel searched, eh?"

"I've no objection to hear reason if I'm spoke to reasonable," said Karen, sulkily; "but I'll not be bullied like a highwayman, when I've my consignment regularly made out, and the freight down in hand, square."

"You may keep your accursed passage-money and welcome," cried Sir Amyas, "so you'll only give me my wife!"

"Show him your certificate," whispered Betty.

Sir Amyas had it ready, and he read it loud enough for all on the Thames to hear. Karen gave a sneering little laugh. "What's that to me? My passenger here has her berth taken in the name of Ann Davis."

"Like enough," said Loveday, "but you remember me, captain, and I can swear that this poor young lady is what his Honour Sir Amyas says. He is a generous young gentleman, and will make it up to you if you are at any loss in the matter."

"A hundred times over!" exclaimed Amyas hotly.

"Hardly that," said Karen. "Van Draagen might have been good for a round hundred if he'd been pleased with the commission."

"I'll give you an order—" began Sir Amyas.

"What have you got about you, sir?" interrupted Karen. "I fancy hard cash better than your orders."

The youth pulled out his purse. There was only a guinea or two and some silver. "One does not go out to parade with much money about one," he said, with a trembling endeavour for a smile, "but if you would send up to my quarters in Whitehall Barracks——"

"Never mind, sir," said Karen, graciously. "I see you are in earnest, and I'll put up with the loss rather than stand in the light of a couple of true lovers. Here, Jack, lend a hand, and we'll hoist the young woman over. She's quiet enough, thanks to Mother Darkness."

The sudden change in tone might perhaps be owing to the skipper's attention having been called by a sign from one of his men to a boat coming up from Woolwich, rowed by men of the Royal navy, who were certain to take part with an officer; but Sir Amyas and Betty were only intent on receiving the inanimate form wrapped up in its mantle. What a meeting it was for Betty, and yet what joy to have her at all! They laid her with her head in her sister's lap, and Sir Amyas hung over her, clasping one of the limp gloved hands, while Eugene called "Aura, Aura," and would have impetuously kissed her awake, but Loveday caught hold of him. "Do not, do not, for pity's sake, little master," she said; "the potion will do her no harm if you let her sleep it off, but she may not know you if you waken her before the time."

"Wretch, what have you given her?" cried Sir Amyas.

"It was not me, sir, it was Mrs. Darke, in a cup of coffee. She vowed it would do no hurt if only she was let to sleep six or eight hours. And see what a misery it has saved her from!"

"That is true," said Betty. "Indeed I believe this is a healthy sleep. See how gently she breathes, how soft and natural her colour is, how cool and fresh her cheek is. I cannot believe there is serious harm done."

"How soon can we reach a physician?" asked Sir Amyas, still anxiously, of the coxswain.

"I can't rightly say, sir," replied he; "but never you fear. They wouldn't do aught to damage such as she."

Patience must perforce be exercised as, now against the tide and the stream, the wherry worked its way back. Once there was a little stir; Sir Amyas instantly hovered over Aurelia, and clasped her hand with a cry of "My dearest life!" The long dark eyelashes slowly rose, the eyes looked up for one moment from his face to her sister's, and then to her brother's, but the lids sank as if weighed down, and with a murmur, "Oh, don't wake me," she turned her face round on Betty's lap and slept again.

"Poor darling, she thinks it a dream," said Betty. "Eugene, do not. Sir, I entreat! Brother, yes, I *will* call you so if you will only let her alone! See how happy and peaceful her dear face is! Do not rouse her into terror and bewilderment."

"If I only were sure she was safe," he sighed, hanging over, with an intensity of affection and anxiety that brought a dew even to the old steersman's eyes; and he kindly engrossed Eugene by telling about the places they passed, and setting him to watch the smart crew of the boat from the Royal Arsenal at Woolwich, which was gaining on them.

Meanwhile the others interrogated Loveday, who told them of the pretext on which Lady Belamour had sent her captive down to Mrs. Darke's. No one save herself had, in my Lady's household, she said, an idea of where the young lady was, Lady Belamour having employed only hired porters except on that night when Lady Aresfield's carriage brought her. This had led to the captivity being known to Lady Belle and her brother, and Loveday had no doubt that it was the discovery of their being aware of it, as well as Jumbo's appearance in the court, that had made her mistress finally decide on this frightful mode of ridding herself of the poor girl. The maid was as adroit a dissembler as her mistress, and she held her peace as to her own part in forwarding Colonel Mar's suit, whether her lady guessed it or not, but she owned with floods of tears how the sight of the young lady's meek and dutiful submission, her quiet trust, and her sweet, simple teaching of the children, had wakened into life again a conscience long dead to all good, and made it impossible to her to carry out this last wicked commission without an attempt to save the creature whom she had learnt to reverence as a saint. Most likely her scruples had been suspected by her mistress, for there had been an endeavour to put it out of her power to give any warning to the victim. Yet after all, the waiting-maid had been too adroit for the lady, or, as she fully owned, Aurelia's firm trust had not been baulked, and deliverance from the lions had come.

CHAPTER XVI.

THE RETURN.

And now the glorious artist, ere he yet
Had reached the Lemnian Isle, limping, returned;
With aching heart he sought his home.
Odyssey—COWPER.

How were they to get the slumbering maiden home? That was the next question. Loveday advised carrying her direct to her old prison, where she would wake without alarm; but Sir Amyas shuddered at the notion, and Betty said she *could* not take her again into a house of Lady Belamour's.

The watermen, who were enthusiastic in the cause, which they understood as that of one young sweetheart rescued by the other, declared that they would carry the sweet lady between them on the cushions of their boat, laid on stretchers; and as they knew of a landing-place near the *Royal York*, with no need of crossing any great thoroughfare, Betty thought this the best chance of taking her sister home without a shock.

The boat from Woolwich had shot London Bridge immediately after them, and stopped at the stairs nearest that where they landed; and just as Sir Amyas, with an exclamation of annoyance at his unserviceable arm, had resigned Aurelia to be lifted on to her temporary litter, a hand was laid on his shoulder, a voice said "Amyas, what means this?" and he found himself face to face with a small, keen-visaged, pale man, with thick grizzled brows overhanging searching dark grey eyes, shaded by a great Spanish hat.

"Sir! oh sir, is it you?" he cried, breathlessly; "now all will be well!"

"I am very glad you think so, Amyas," was the grave answer; "for all this has a strange appearance."

"It is my dearest wife, sir, my wife, whom I

have just recovered after—Oh, say, sir, if you think all is well with her, and it is only a harmless sleeping potion. Sister—Betty—this is my good father, Mr. Wayland. He is as good as a physician. Let him see my sweetest life."

Mr. Wayland bent over the slumbering figure still in the bottom of the boat, heard what could be told of the draught by Loveday, whom he recognized as his wife's attendant, and feeling Aurelia's pulse, said, "I should not think there was need for fear. To the outward eye she is a model of sleeping innocence." "Well you may say so," and "She is indeed," broke from the baronet and the waiting-maid at the same instant; but Mr. Wayland heeded them little as he impatiently asked, "Where and how is your mother, Amyas?"

"In health, sir, at home, I suppose," said Sir Amyas; "but oh, sir, hear me, before you see her."

"I must, if you walk with me," said Mr. Wayland, turning for a moment to bid his servant reward and dismiss his boat's crew, and see to the

VOL. II.   S

transport of his luggage; and in the meantime Aurelia was lifted by her bearers.

Sir Amyas again uttered a rejoicing, "We feared you were in the hands of the pirates, sir."

"So I was; but the governor of Gibraltar obtained my release, and was good enough to send me home direct in a vessel on the king's service," said Mr. Wayland, taking the arm his stepson offered to assist his lameness. "Now for your explanation, Amyas; only let me hear first that my babes are well."

"Yes, sir, all well. You had my letter?"

"Telling of that strange disguised wedding? I had, the very day I was captured."

By the time they had come to the place where their ways parted, Mr. Wayland had heard enough to be so perplexed and distressed that he knew not that he had been drawn out of the way to Hanover Square, till at the entrance of the *Royal York*, they found Betty asseverating to the landlady that she was bringing no case of small pox into the house; and showing, as a passport of admittance, two little dents on the white wrist and temple.

At that instant the sound brought Major Delavie hurrying from his sitting-room at his best speed. There was a look of horror on his face as he saw his daughter's senseless condition, but Betty sprang to his side to prevent his wakening her, and Aurelia was safely carried up stairs and laid upon her sister's bed, still sleeping, while Betty and Loveday unloosed her clothes. Her bearers were sent for refreshment to the bar, and the gentlemen stood looking on one another in the sitting-room, Mr. Wayland utterly shocked, incredulous of the little he did understand, and yet unable to go home until he should hear more; and the Major hardly less horrified, in the midst of his relief. "But where's Belamour?" he cried. "Your uncle, I mean."

"Where?" said Sir Amyas. "They said he was gone out."

"So they told me! And see here!"

Major Delavie produced Lady Belamour's note.

"A blind!" cried Sir Amyas, turning away under a strange stroke of pain and shame. "Oh! mother, mother!" and he dashed out of the room.

Poor Mr. Wayland sat down as one who could stand no longer. "Of what do they suspect her?" he said hoarsely.

"Sir," said the good Major, "I grieve sincerely for and with you. Opposition to this match with my poor child seems to have transported my poor cousin to strange and frantic lengths, but you may trust me to shield and guard her from exposure as far as may be."

Her husband only answered by a groan, and wrung Major Delavie's hand, but their words were interrupted by Sir Amyas's return. He had been to his uncle's chamber, and had found on the table a note addressed to the Major. Within was an inclosure directed to A. Belamour, Esq.

"If you have found the way to the poor captive, for pity's sake come to her rescue. Be in the court with your faithful black by ten o'clock, and you may yet save one who loves and looks to you."

On the outer sheet was written—

"I distrust this handwriting, and suspect a ruse. In case I do not return, send for Hargrave,

Sandy's, Godfrey, as witnesses to my sanity, and storm the fair one's fortress in person. A. B."

"It is not my Aurelia's writing," said the Major. "Bravest of friends, what has he not dared on her account!"

"This is too much!" cried Mr. Wayland, striving in horror against his convictions. "I cannot hear my beloved wife loaded with monstrous suspicions in her absence!"

"I am sorry to say this is no new threat ever since poor Belamour has crossed her path," said the Major.

"What have you done, sir?" asked Sir Amyas.

"I fear I have but wasted time," said the Major. "I have been to Hanover Square, and getting no admittance there, I came back in the hope you might be on the track with Betty—as, thank God, you were! The first thing to be done now is to find what she has done with Belamour," he added, rising up.

"That must fall to my share," said Mr. Wayland, pale and resolute. "Come with me, Amyas, your young limbs will easily return before the effect of the narcotic has passed, and I need fuller explanation."

Stillness then came on the Delavie party. The Major went up stairs, and sat by Aurelia's bed gazing with eyes dazzled with tears at the child he had so longed to see, and whom he found again in this strange trance. A doctor came, and quite confirmed Mr. Wayland's opinion, that the drug would not prove deleterious, provided the sleep was not disturbed, and Betty continued her watch, after hearing what her father knew of Mr. Belamour. She was greatly struck with the self-devotion that had gone with open eyes into so dreadful a snare as a madhouse of those days rather than miss the least chance of saving Aurelia.

"If we go by perils dared, the uncle is the true knight-errant," said she to her father. "I wonder which our child truly loves the best!"

"Betty!" said her father, scandalised.

"Ay, I know, Sir Amyas is a charming boy, but what a boy he is! And she has barely spoken with him or seen him, whereas Mr. Belamour has been kind to her for a whole twelvemonth. I know what I should do if I were in her place. I would declare that I intended to be married to the uncle, and would keep to it!"

"He would think it base to put the question."

"He would; but indeed, dear sir, I think it would be but right and due to the dear child herself that she should have her free choice, and not be bound for ever by a deception! Yes, I know the poor boy's despair would be dreadful, but it would be better for them both than such a mistake."

"Hush! I hear him knocking at the door, you cruel woman."

The bedroom opened into the parlour the party had hired, so that both could come out and meet Sir Amyas with the door ajar, without relaxing their watch upon the sleeper. The poor young man looked pale, shocked, and sorrowful. "Well," said he, after having read in their looks that there was no change, "he knows the worst." Then, on a further token of interrogation, "It may have been my fault; I took him, unannounced, through the whole suite of rooms, and in the closet at the end, with all the doors open, she was having an altercation with Mar. He was insisting on knowing what she had done with"—(he signed towards the other room) " she, upbraiding him with faithlessness. They were deaf to an approach, till Mr. Wayland, in a loud voice, ordered me back, saying ' it was no scene for a son.' "

" I trust it will not end in a challenge ? " asked the Major, gravely.

" No, my father's infirmity renders him no fighting man, and I—I may not challenge my superior officer."

" But your uncle ? " said Betty, much fearing that such a scene might have led to his being forgotten.

" I should have told you. We had not made many steps from hence before we met poor Jumbo wandering like a dog that had lost his master. Mr. Belamour had taken the precaution of giving Jumbo the pass-key, and not taking him into that house (some day I will pull every brick of it down), so he watched till by and by he saw a coach come out with all the windows closed, and as his master had bidden him in such a case, he kept along on the pavement near, and never lost sight of it till he had tracked it right across the City to a house with iron-barred windows inside a high wall. There it went in, and he could not follow, but he asked the people what place it was, and though they jeered at him, he made out that it was as we feared. Nay, do not be alarmed, sister, he will soon be with us. My poor father shut me out, and I know not what passed with my mother, but just as I could wait no longer to return to my dearest life, he came out and told me that he had found out that my uncle was in a house at Moorfields, and he is gone himself to liberate him. He is himself a justice of the peace, and he will call for Dr. Sandys by the way, that there may be no difficulty. He is gone in the coach-and-four, with Jumbo on the box, so that matters will soon be righted."

"And a heroic champion set free," said Betty, moving to return to her sister, when the others would not be denied having another look at the sweet slumberer, on whose face there was now a smile as if her dreams were marvellously lovely;

or, as Betty thought, as if she knew their voices even in her sleep.

Sir Amyas had not seen his mother again. He only knew that Mr. Wayland had come out with a face as of one stricken to the heart, a sad contrast to that which had greeted him an hour before, and while the carriage was coming round, had simply said, "I did wrong to leave her."

It would not bear being talked over, and both son and kinsman took refuge in silence. Two hours more of this long day had passed, and then a coach stopped at the door. Sir Amyas hurried down in his eager anxiety, and came back with his uncle, holding him by the hand like a child, in his gladness, and Betty came out to meet them in the outer room with a face of grateful welcome and outstretched hands.

"Sir! sir! you have done more than all of us."

"Yet you and your young champion here were the victors," said Mr. Belamour.

"Ah, we dared and suffered nothing like you."

"I hope you did not suffer much," said the Major, looking at the calm face and neatly-tied white hair, which seemed to have suffered no disarrangement.

"No," said Mr. Belamour, smiling, "my little friend Eugene, ay, and my nephew himself, are hoping to hear I was released from fetters and a heap of straw, but I took care to give them no opportunity. I merely told them they were under a mistake, and had better take care. I gave them a reference or two, but I saw plainly that was of no use, though they promised to send, and then I did exactly as they bade me, so as to deprive them of all excuse for meddling with me, letting them know that I could pay for decent treatment so long as I was in their hands."

"Did you receive it?"

"I was told in a mild manner, adapted to my intelligence, that if I behaved well, I might eat at the master's table, and have a room with only one inmate. Of the former I have not an engaging experience, either as to the fare, the hostess, or the company. Of the latter, happily I know little, as I only know that my comrade was to be a harmless gibbering idiot; of good birth, poor fellow. However, the sounds I heard, and the court I looked into, convinced me that my privileges were worth paying for."

He spoke very quietly, but he shuddered involuntarily, and Betty, unable to restrain her tears, retreated to her sister's side.

CHAPTER XVII.

WAKING.

So Love was still the Lord of all.—SCOTT.

THE summer sun was sinking and a red glow was on the wall above Aurelia's head when she moved again, upon the shutting of the door, while supper was being taken by the gentlemen in the outer room.

Presently her lips moved, and she said, "Sister," not in surprise, but as if she thought herself at home, and as Betty gently answered, "Yes, my darling child," the same voice added, "I have had such a dream; I thought I was a chrysalis, and that I could not break my shell nor spread my wings."

"You can now, my sweet," said Betty, venturing to kiss her.

Recollection came. "Sister Betty, is it you indeed?" and she threw her arms round Betty's neck, clinging tight to her in delicious silence, till she raised her head and said: "No, this is not home. Oh, is it all true?"

"True that I have you again, my dear, dearest, sweetest child," said Betty. "Oh, thank God for it."

"Thank God," repeated Aurelia. "Now I have you nothing will be dreadful. But where am I? I thought once I was in a boat with you and Eugene, and some one else. Was it a dream? I can't remember anything since that terrible old woman made me drink the coffee. You have not come there, have you?"

"No, dear child, it was no dream that you were in a boat. We had been searching everywhere for you, and we were bringing you back sound, sound asleep," said Betty, in her tenderness speaking as if to a little child.

"I knew you would," said Aurelia; "I knew God would save me. Love is strong as death, you know," she added dreamily: "I think I felt it all round me in that sleep."

"That was what you murmured once or twice in your sleep," said Betty.

"And now, oh! it is so sweet to lie here and know it is you. And wasn't *he* there too?"

"Sir Amyas? Yes, my dear. He came for you. He and my father and the others are in the other room waiting for you to wake."

"I hear their voices," cried Aurelia, with a start, sitting up. "Oh! that's my papa's voice! Oh! how good it is to hear it!"

"I will call him as soon as I have set you a little in order. Are you sure you are well, my dearest? No headache?"

"Quite, quite well! Why, sister, I have not been ill; and if I had, I should skip to see you, and hear their voices, only I wish they would speak louder! That's Eugene! Oh! they are hushing him. Let me make haste," and she moved with an alacrity that was most reassuring. "But I can't understand. Is it morning or evening?"

"Evening, my dear. They are at supper. Are not you hungry?"

"Oh, yes, I believe I am;" but as she was about to wash her hands: "My rings, where are they?

My rings, my wedding-ring? Look in my glove!"

"No, they are not there. My dear, they must have robbed you! And oh! Aurelia, what have you done to your hair?"

"My hair? It was all there this morning. Sister, it was that woman, I remember now, I was not quite sound asleep, but I had no power to move or cry out, and the woman was snipping and Loveday crying."

"Vile creature!" burst out Betty.

"My hair will grow!" said Aurelia; "but I had so guarded my wedding-ring—and what will he, Sir Amyas, think?"

Their voices were at this moment heard, and in another second Aurelia was held against her father's breast, as in broken words he sobbed out thanks for her restoration, and implored her pardon for having trusted her out of his care.

"Oh! sir, do not speak so! Dear papa, I have tried hard to do you no harm, and to behave well. Please, sir, give me your blessing."

"God bless you indeed, my child. He has blessed you in guarding you as your innocence deserved, though I did not. Ah! others are impatient. The poor old father comes second now."

After a few minutes spent in repairing the disorder of her dress, and her hands in those of her father and little brother, she was led to the outer room where in the twilight there was a rapturous rush, an embrace, a fondling of the hand in the manner more familiar to her than the figure from before whom it proceeded. She only said in her gentle plaintive tone, "Oh, sir, it was not my fault. They took away your rings."

"Nay," said a voice, new to her, "here are your rings, Lady Belamour. I must trust to your Christian charity to pardon her who caused you to be stripped of them."

The name of Lady Belamour made her start as that of her enemy, but a truly familiar tone said, "You need not fear, my kind friend. This is Mr. Wayland, who, to our great joy, has returned, and has come to restore your jewels."

"Indeed I am very glad yours is not lost," said Aurelia, not a little bewildered.

Mr. Wayland said a few words of explanation that his wife's agent at Greenwich had brought them back to her.

"Pray let me have them," entreated Sir Amyas; "I must put them on again!"

"Stay," said Major Delavie; "I can have such things done only under true colours and in the full light of day. The child is scarcely awake yet, and does not know one from the other! Why neither of you so much as know the colour of the eyes of the other! Can you tell me, sir?"

"Heavenly," exclaimed the youth, in an ecstatic tone of self-defence, which set the Major laughing and saying, "My silly maid knows as little which gentleman put on the ring."

"I do, sir," said Aurelia indignantly; "I know his voice and hand quite well," and in the impulse she quitted her father's arm and put both hands into those of her young adorer, saying, "Pray sir, pardon me, I never thought to hurt you so cruelly."

There was a cry of, "My own, my dearest life," and she was clasped as she had been immediately after her strange wedding.

However, the sound of a servant's step made them separate instantly, and Betty begged that the supper might not be removed, since it was many hours since her sister had tasted food.

Sir Amyas and Betty hovered about her, giving her whatever she could need, in the partial light, while the others stood apart, exchanging such explanations as they could. Mr. Wayland said he must report himself to Government on the morrow; but intended afterwards to take his wife to Bowstead, whither she had sent all her children with Mrs. Dove. There was a great tenderness in his tone as he spoke of her, and when he took leave Mr. Belamour shrugged his shoulders, saying, "She will come round him again!"

"It is true enough that he ought not to have left her to herself," said the Major.

"You making excuses for her after the diabolical plot of to-day?" said Mr. Belamour; "I could forgive her all but that letter to you."

"My Lady loves her will," quoted the Major; "it amounts to insanity in some women, I believe."

"So I might say does men's infatuation towards women like her," muttered Mr. Belamour.

By this time Aurelia had finished her meal, and Betty was anxious to carry her off without any more excitement, for she was still drowsy and confused. She bade her father good night, asking his blessing as of old, but when Mr. Belamour kissed her hand and repeated the good night, she said, "Sir, I ought to have trusted you; I am so sorry."

"It is all well now, my child," he said, soothingly, understanding Betty's wish; "Sleep, and we will talk it over."

So the happy sisters once more slept in each other's arms, till in the early summer morning Betty heard the whole story from Aurelia, now fully herself, though she slumbered again after all was poured into her sister's bosom.

Betty had sympathised step by step, and felt even more strongly than Harriet that the situation had been intolerable for womanhood, and that only

Aurelia's childishness could have endured it so long. Only the eldest sister held that it would have been right and honourable to have spoken before flashing out the flame; but when, with many tears of contrition, Aurelia owned that she had long thought so, and longed to confess it, what could the motherly sister do but kiss the tears away, and rejoice that the penance was over which had been borne with such constancy and self-devotion.

Then Betty rose quietly, and after giving thanks on her knees that the gentle spirit had passed through all unscathed, untainted with even the perception of evil, she applied herself to the adaptation of one of her morning caps to her poor shorn lamb's head. Nor did Aurelia wake again till her father came to the door to make sure that all was well with his recovered treasure, and to say that Loveday would recover for her the box of clothes, which old Madge had hidden.

Loveday had gone back to her mistress, who either had not discovered her betrayal, or, as things had turned out, could not resent it.

So, fresh and blooming, Aurelia came out into the sitting-room, whence her father held out his arms to her. He would have her all to himself for a little while, since even Eugene was gone to his daily delight, the seeing the changing of the guard.

"And now, my child, tell me," he said, when he had heard a little of her feelings through these adventures, "what would you have me do? Remember, such a wedding as yours goes for nothing, and you are still free to choose either or neither of your swains."

"Oh, papa!" in a remonstrating tone.

"You were willing to wed your old hermit?"

"I was content *then*. He was very kind to me."

"Content then, eh? Suppose you were told he was your real husband?"

"Sir, he is not!" cried Aurelia, frightened.

"If he were?"

"I would try to do my duty," she said, in a choked voice.

"Silly child, don't cry. And how, if after these fool's tricks it turns out that the other young spark is bound to that red-faced little spitfire and cannot have you?"

"Papa, don't!" she cried. "You know he is my husband in my heart, and always will be, and if he cannot come back to me take me home, and I will try to be a good daughter to you," and she hid her face on his shoulder.

"Poor child, it is a shame to tease her," said her father, raising up her face; "I only wanted to know which of them you would wish to put on the ring again. I see. You need not be afraid, you shall have that ruby one; but as for the little gold one, wait for that till it is put on in church, my dear. Ah! and there's the flutter of his wings, or rather the rattle of his spurs. Now then, young people, you shall not be hindered from a full view of each other's lineaments. It is the first time you ever had a real sight of each other, neither of you being in a swoon, is it not? I trust you do not repent upon fuller acquaintance. Aurelia got as far as the shoe-buckles once, I believe."

"She will get no farther this time, sir, if you

annihilate her with your pleasantry," said Betty, fully convinced by this time.

"Ah! young Love has made himself more dazzling than ever," continued the Major, too delighted to be stopped. "The fullest dress uniform, I declare; M. le Capitaine is bent on doing honour to the occasion."

"Would that it were on for no other reason, sir," said Sir Amyas; "but the King and Queen have taken it into their heads to go off to Kew, and here am I under orders to command the escort. I verily believe it is all spite on the Colonel's part, for Russell would have exchanged the turn with me, but he sent down special orders for me. I have but half an hour to spend here, and when I shall be able to get back again Heaven only knows."

However, he and Aurelia were permitted to improve that half hour to the utmost in their own way, while the Major and Betty were reading a long and characteristic letter from Mrs. Arden, inquiring certainly for her sister's fate, but showing far more solicitude in proving that she (Harriet Arden) had acted a wise, prudent, and sisterly part, and that it was most unreasonable and cruel to treat her as accountable for her sister's disappearance. It was really making her quite ill, and Mr. Arden was like a man—so disagreeable about it.

Betty was very glad this epistle had not come till it was possible to laugh at it. She would have sat down to reply to it at once, had not a billet been brought in from the widow of one of her father's old brother officers who had heard of his being in town, and begged him to bring his daughter to see her, excusing herself for not waiting on Miss Delavie, as she was very feeble and infirm.

It was a request that could not be refused, but Aurelia was not equipped for such a visit, and shrank timidly from showing herself. So when Mr. Belamour came down it was agreed that she should remain at home under his protection, in which she could be very happy, though his person was as strange to her as his voice was familiar. Indeed she felt as if a burden was on her mind till she could tell him of her shame at having failed in the trust and silence that he had enjoined on her.

"My child," he said, "we have carried it too far. It was more than we ought to have required of you, and I knew it. I had made up my mind, and told my nephew that the first time you really asked I should tell the whole truth, and trust to your discretion, while of course he wished for nothing more."

"As my sister said, it was my fault."

"Nay, I think you had good cause to stand on your defence, and I cannot have you grieve over it. You have shown an unshaken steadiness under trial since, such as ought indeed to be compensation."

"I deserved it all," said Aurelia; "and I do hope that I am a little wiser and less foolish for it all; a little more of a woman," she added, blushing.

"A soul trained by love and suffering, as in the old legend," said Mr. Belamour thoughtfully.

Thoroughly pleasant was her *tête-à-tête* with

him, especially when she artlessly asked him whether her dear sister were not all she had told him, and he fervently answered that indeed she was "a perfect lesson to all so-called beauties of what the true loveliness of a countenance can be."

"Oh, I am so glad," cried Aurelia. "I never saw a face—a woman's, I mean—that I liked as well as my dear sister's!"

She was sorry when they were interrupted by a call from Mr. Wayland, who had reported himself at the Secretary at War, but could do no more that day, and had come to inquire for her. He and Mr. Belamour drew apart into a window, and conversed in a low voice, and then they came to her, and Mr. Wayland desired to know from her where she found the recipe for the cosmetic which had nearly cost her so dearly.

"It was in a shelf in the wainscoting, in a sort of little study, at that house," said Aurelia.

"Among other papers?"

"Quantities of other papers."

"Of what kind?"

"Letters, and bills, and wills, and parchments! Oh, so dusty! Some were on paper tumbling to pieces, and some on tiny slips of parchment."

"And you read them all?"

"I had to read them to see what they were, as well as I could make out, and I sorted them and tied them up in bundles."

"Can you tell me whether they were Delavie wills?"

"I should think they were. I know that the oldest of all were Latin, and I could make nothing out in them but something about *Manoriem* and Carminster, and what looked like the names of some of the fields at home."

"Do you think you could show me those slips?"

"I do not suppose any one has touched them."

"Then, my dear young lady, you would confer a great favour on me if you would allow Mr. Belamour and myself to escort you to Delavie House and show us these papers. I fear it may be alarming and distressing."

"Oh no, sir, I know no harm can happen to me where Mr. Belamour is," she said smiling.

"It may be very important," he said, and she went to put on her hood.

"Surely," said Mr. Wayland, "the title-deeds cannot have been left there?"

"No. The title-deeds to the main body of the property are at Hargrave's. I have seen them, at the time of my brother's marriage; but still this may be what was wanting."

"Yet the sending this child to search is a presumption that no such document existed."

"Of course no one supposed it did," said Mr. Wayland, on the defence again.

Aurelia was quickly ready in her little hood and kerchief, and trim high-heeled shoes. She was greatly surprised to find how near she had been to her friends during these last few days of her captivity, and when Madge obeyed the summons to the door, the old woman absolutely smiled to see her safe, and the little terrier danced about her in such transports that she begged to take him back with her.

She opened the door of the little empty book room, where nothing stood except the old bureau.

That, she said, had been full of letters, but all the oldest things had been within a door opening in the wainscot, which she should never have found had not Bob pushed it open in his search for rats, and then she found a tin case full of papers and parchments, much older, she thought, than the letters. She had tied them up together, and easily produced them.

Mr. Wayland handed them to Mr. Belamour, whose legal eye was better accustomed to crabbed old documents. A conversation that had begun on the way about Fay and Letty was resumed, and interested both their father and Aurelia so much that they forgot to be impatient, until Mr. Belamour looked up from his examination, saying, "This is what was wanting. Here is a grant in the 12th year of Henry III. to Guglielmus ab Vitâ and the heirs male of his body of the Manor, lying without the city of Carminster, and here are three wills of successive lords of Delavie expressly mentioning heirs male. Now the deeds that I have seen do not go beyond 1539, when Henry Delavie had a grant of the Grange and lands belonging to Carminster Abbey—the place, in fact, where the Great House stands, and there is in that no exclusion of female heirs. But the Manor house can certainly be proved to be entailed in the male line alone, according to what was, I believe, the tradition of the family."

"There is no large amount of property involved, I fear," said Mr. Wayland.

"There is an old house, much out of repair, and a few farms worth, may be, £200 a year, a loss that will not be material to you, sir, I hope."

"Do you mean — ?" said Aurelia, not daring to ask farther.

"I mean, my dear young lady," said Mr. Wayland, "that your researches have brought to light the means of doing tardy justice to your good father."

"His right to the Manor House is here established," explained Mr. Belamour. "It will not be a matter of favour of my Lady's, but, as my brother supposed, he ought to have been put in possession on the old Lord's death."

"And Eugene will be a gentleman of estate,"

cried Aurelia, joyously. "Nor will any one be able to drive out my dear father! Oh! how happy I am."

Both she and Mr. Belamour spared Mr. Wayland the knowledge of my Lady's many broken promises, and indeed she was anxious to get back to the *Royal York*, lest her father and sister should have returned, and think her again vanished.

They all met at the door, and much amazed were the Major and Betty to encounter her with her two squires. Mr. Wayland took the Major to show him the parchments. Betty had her explanation from her sister and Mr. Belamour.

"You actually ventured back to that dreadful house," she said, looking at them gratefully.

"You see what protectors I had," said Aurelia, with a happy smile.

"Yes," said Betty, "I have been longing to say —only I cannot," for she was almost choked by a great sob, "how very much we owe to you, sir. I could say it better if I did not feel it so much." And she held out her hand.

"You cannot owe to me a tithe of what I owe

to your sister," said Mr. Belamour, "and through her to you, madam. Much as nature had done for her, never would she have been to the miserable recluse the life and light-bringing creature she was, save for the 'sister' she taught me to know and love, even before I saw her."

A wonderful revelation here burst on Aurelia, the at least half-married woman, and she fled precipitately, smiling to herself in ecstasy, behind her great fan.

Betty, never dreaming of the drift of the words, so utterly out of the reach of love did she suppose herself, replied, composedly, "Our Aurelia is a dear good girl, and I am thankful that through all her trials she has so proved herself. I am glad she has been a comfort to you, sir. She——"

"And will not you complete the cure, and render the benefit lasting?" said Mr. Belamour, who had never let go the hand she had given him in gratitude, and now gave it a pressure that conveyed, for the first time, his meaning.

"Oh!" she cried, trying to take it away, "your

kindness and gratitude are leading you too far, sir. A hideous old fright like me, instead of a lovely young thing like her! It is an absurdity."

"Stay, Miss Delavie. Remember that your Aurelia's roses and lilies were utterly wasted on me; I never thought whether she was beautiful save when others raved about her. I never saw her till yesterday; but the voice, the goodness, the amiability, in fact all that I did truly esteem and prize in her I had already found matured and mellowed together with that beauty of countenance which is independent of mere skin-deep complexion and feature. You know my history, and how far I am from being able to offer you a fresh untouched young heart, such as my nephew brings to the fair Aurelia; but the devotion of my life will be yours if you will accept it."

"Sir, I cannot listen to you. You are very good, but I can never leave my father. Oh, let me go away!"

CHAPTER XVIII.

MAKING THE BEST OF IT.

> At last the Queen said, " Girl, I bid thee rise,
> For now thou hast found favour in mine eyes,
> And I repent me of the misery
> That in this place thou hast endured of me,
> Altho' because of it the joy indeed
> Shall now be mine, that pleasure is thy meed."
> MORRIS.

THOSE were evil times, and the court examples were most corrupting, so that a splendid and imperious woman like Urania, Lady Belamour, had found little aid from public opinion when left to herself by the absence of her second husband. Selfish, unscrupulous, and pleasure-loving she was by nature, but during Sir Jovian Belamour's lifetime she had been kept within bounds. Then came a brief widowhood, when debt and difficulty hurried her into accepting Mr. Wayland, a thoughtful scientific man, whose wealth had accumulated without much volition of his own to an extent that made her covet his alliance. Enthralled by her charm of manner, he had not awakened to the perception of what she really was during the few years that had elapsed before he was sent abroad, and she refused to accompany him.

Then it was that wealth larger than she had before commanded, and a court appointment, involved her in more dangerous habits. Her debts, both of extravagance and of the gaming table, were enormous, trenching hard on the Delavie property, and making severe inroads on Mr. Wayland's means; but the Belamour estates being safely tied up, she had only been able to borrow on her dower. She had sinned with a high hand, after the fashion of the time, and then, in terror at the approaching return of her husband, had endeavoured to conceal the ravages of her extravagance by her bargain for her son's hand.

The youth, bred up at a distance, and then the companion of his step-father, had on his return found his home painfully altered in his two years' absence, and had been galled and grieved by the state of things, so that even apart from the clearing of his prospects, the relief was great. The quarrel with Colonel Mar that Mr. Wayland had interrupted was not made up. There was no opportunity, for Mr. Wayland at once removed his family to Bowstead, there to remain while he transacted his business in London.

Moreover Mr. Belamour and Mr. Wayland agreed in selling the young baronet's commission. The Major allowed that it was impossible that he should remain under the command of his present Colonel, but regretted that he should not continue in the service, declaring it the best school for a young man, and that he did not want to see his son-in-law a muddle-brained sporting country squire. He would have had Sir Amyas exchange into the line, and see a little service before settling down, but Maria Theresa had not as yet set Europe in a blaze, and in the absence of a promising war Sir Amyas did more incline to his uncle's representations of duties to tenants and to his country, and was even ready to prepare himself for them when he should be of sufficient age to undertake them. However, in the midst of the debates a new scheme was made. Mr.

Belamour had been called upon and welcomed by his old friends, who, being men of rank and influence, had risen in life while he was immured at Bowstead. One of these had just received a diplomatic appointment at Vienna, and in spite of insular ignorance of foreign manners was at a loss for a capable suite. Mr. Belamour suggested Major Delavie, as from his long service in Austria likely to be very useful. The Envoy caught at the idea, and the thought of once more seeing his old comrades enchanted the Major, whose only regret was that his hero, Prince Eugene, had been dead three years; but to visit his grave would be something. Appointments ran in families, so that nothing could be easier than to obtain one for the young baronet; and though Mr. Belamour did not depend on his own health enough to accept anything, he was quite willing to join the party, and to spend a little time abroad, while his nephew was growing somewhat older, making an essay of his talents, and at any rate putting off the commencement of stagnation. Thus matters settled themselves, the only disappointed member of the family being Mrs. Arden, who thought it very hard that she could not stir any one up to request an appointment of her husband as chaplain—not even himself!

Mr. Wayland was at once called upon to go out to America to superintend the defences of the Canadian frontier, and he resolved on taking his family out, obtaining land, and settling there permanently. He would pay all my Lady's debts, but she should never again appear in London society, and cruel exile as it must seem to her, he trusted that his affection and tenderness would in time reconcile her to the new way of life, knowing as she did that he had forgiven much that had made him look like a crushed and sorrowful man in the midst of all the successes and the honours he received from his country.

She remained quietly at Bowstead, and none of them saw her except her son and the Major, to the latter of whom her husband brought a message that she would esteem it a favour if he would come and visit her there, the day before he returned to Carminster. Very much affected, the good Major complied with her request, went down with Mr. Wayland and spent a night at Bowstead.

He found that she had accepted her fate with

the good grace of a woman whose first instinct was not to make herself disagreeable. She was rather pale, and not "made up" in any way, but exquisitely though more simply dressed, and more beautiful than ever, her cousin thought, as he always did whenever he came into her presence. She was one of those people whose beauty is always a fresh surprise, and she was far more self-possessed than he was.

"So, Cousin Harry, where am I to begin my congratulations! I did you an unwitting service when I sent your daughter to search among those musty old parchments. I knew my father believed in the existence of some such document, but I thought all those hoards in Delavie House were devoid of all legal importance, and had been sifted again and again. Besides, I always meant to settle that old house upon you."

"I have always heard so, cousin," he answered.

"But it was such a mere trifle," she added, "that it never seemed worth while to set the lawyers to work about that alone, so I waited for other work to be in hand."

"There is a homely Scottish proverb, my Lady,

which declares that the scrapings of the muckle pot are worth the wee pot fu'. A mere trifle to you is affluence to us."

"I am sincerely rejoiced at it, Harry" (no doubt she thought she was), "you will keep up the old name, while my scrupulous lord and master gives up my poor patrimony to the extortionate creditors for years to come. It is well that the young lovers have other prospects. So Harry, you see, after all, I kept my word, and your daughter is provided for," she continued with an arch smile. "Pretty creature, I find my son bears me more malice than she does for the robbery that was perpetrated on her. It was too tempting, Harry. Nature will repair her loss, but at our time of life we must beg, borrow, or steal."

"That was the least matter," said the Major gravely.

"This is the reason why I wished to see you," said my Lady, laying her white hand on his, "I wanted to explain."

"Cousin, cousin, had not you better leave it alone?" said Major Delavie. "You know you can always talk a poor man out of his senses at the moment."

"Yet listen, Harry, and understand my troubles. Here was I pledged, absolutely pledged, to give my son to Lady Aresfield's daughter. I do not know whether she may not yet sue me for breach of contract, though Wayland has repaid her the loans she advanced me; and on the other hand, in spite of all my precautions, Mar had obtained a sight of your poor daughter, and I knew him well enough to be aware that to put her entirely and secretly out of his reach was the only chance of preserving her from his pursuit. I had excellent accounts of the worthy man to whom I meant her to be consigned, and I knew that when she wrote to you as a West Indian queen you would be able to forgive your poor cousin. I see what you would say, but sending her to you was impossible, since I had to secure her both from Amyas and from Mar. It would only have involved you in perplexities innumerable, and might have led even to bloodshed! I may not have acted wisely, but weak women in difficulties know not which path to choose."

"There is always the straight one," said he.

"Ah! you strong men can easily say so, but

for us poor much-tried women! However," she said, suddenly changing her tone, " Love has checkmated us, and I rejoice. Your daughter will support the credit of the name! I am glad the new Lady Belamour will not be that little termagant milkmaid Belle, whom circumstances compelled me to inflict upon my poor boy! The title will be your daughter's alone. I have promised my husband that in the New World I will sink into plain Mrs. Wayland." Then with a burst of genuine feeling she exclaimed, " He *is* a good man, Harry."

"He is indeed, Urania, I believe you will yet be happier than you have ever been."

"What, among barbarians who never saw a loo-table, and get the modes three months too late! And you are laughing at me, but you see I am a poor frivolous being, not sufficient to myself like your daughters! They say Aurelia was as sprightly as a spring butterfly all the time she was shut up at Bowstead with no company save the children and old Belamour!"

"They are lovely children, madam, Aurelia dotes on them, and you will soon find them all you need."

"Their father is never weary of telling me so. He is never so happy as when they hang about him and tell him of Cousin Aura, or Sister Aura as they love to call her."

"It was charming to see them dance round her when he brought them to spend the day with her. Mr. Wayland brought his good kinswoman, who will take charge of them on the voyage, and Aurelia was a little consoled at the parting by seeing how tender and kind she is with them."

"Aye! If I do not hate that woman it will be well, for she is as much a duenna for me as governess for the children! Heigh-ho! what do not our follies bring on us? We poor creatures should never be left to the great world."

The pretty air of repentance was almost irresistible, well as the Major knew it for the mood of the moment, assumed as what would best satisfy him.

"I rejoice," she went on, "in spite of my lovely daughter-in-law's discretion, she will be well surrounded with guardians. Has the excellent Betty consented?"

"At last, madam. My persuasions were vain

till she found that Mr. Belamour would gladly come with us to Austria, and that she should be enabled to watch over both her young sister and me."

"There, again, I give myself credit, Harry. Would the sacred flame ever have awakened in yonder misanthrope had I not sent your daughter to restore him to life?" She spoke playfully, but the Major could not help thinking she had persuaded herself that all his present felicity was owing to her benevolence, and that she would persuade him of it too, if she went on much longer looking at him so sweetly. He *would* not tax her with the wicked note she had written to account for Mr. Belamour's disappearance, and which she had forgotten; he felt that he could not impel one, whom he could not but still regard with tenderness, to utter any more untruths and excuses.

"By the by," she added, "does your daughter take my waiting-maid after all? I would have forgiven her, for she is an admirable hairdresser, but Wayland says he cannot have so ingenious a person in his house; though after all I do not see that she is a bit worse than others of her condition, and she herself insists on trying to become

Aurelia's attendant, vowing that the sight of her is as good as any Methodist sermon!"

"Precisely, madam. We were all averse to taking her with us, but Aurelia said she owed her much gratitude; and she declared so earnestly that the sight of my dear child brought back all the virtuous and pious thoughts she had forgotten, that even Betty's heart was touched, and she is to go with us, on trial."

"Oh! she is as honest as regards money and jewels as ever I knew a waiting-maid, but for the rest!" Lady Belamour shrugged her shoulders. "However, one is as good as another, and at least she will never let her lady go a fright! See here, Harry. These are the Delavie jewels: I shall never need them more: carry them to your daughters."

"Nay, your own daughters, Urania."

"Never mind the little wretches. Their father will provide for them, and they will marry American settlers in the forests. What should they do with court jewels? It is his desire. See here, this suit of pearls is what I wore at my wedding with Amyas's father, I should like Aurelia to be married in them. Farewell, Harry, you did better for yourself than if you had taken me. Yet maybe I might have been a better woman——" She stopped short as she looked at his honest face, and eyes full of tears.

"No, Urania," he said, "man's love could not have done for you what only another Love can do. May you yet find that and true Life."

The sisters were not married at the same time. Neither Mr. Belamour nor his Elizabeth could endure to make part of the public pageant that it was thought well should mark the *real* wedding at Bowstead. So their banns were put up at St. Clement Danes, and one quiet morning they slipped out, with no witnesses but the Major, Aurelia, and Eugene, and were wedded there in the most unobtrusive manner.

As to the great marriage, a month later at Bowstead, there was a certain bookseller named Richardson, who by favour of Hargrave got a view of it, and who is thought there to have obtained some ideas for the culminating wedding of his great novel.

A little later, the following letter was written

from the excellent Mrs. Montagu to her correspondent Mrs. Elizabeth Carter. "There was yesterday presented, preparatory to leaving England for Vienna, the young Lady Belamour, incomparably the greatest beauty who has this year appeared at Court. Every one is running after her, but she appears perfectly unconscious of the *furore* she has excited, and is said to have been bred up in all simplicity in the country, and to be as good as she is fair. Her young husband, Sir Amyas Belamour, is a youth of much promise, and they seem absolutely devoted, with eyes only for each other. They are said to have gone through a series of adventures as curious as they are romantic; and indeed, when they made their appearance, there was a general whisper, begun by young Mr. Horace Walpole, of

"Cupid and Psyche."

www.ingramcontent.com/pod-product-compliance
Lightning Source LLC
Chambersburg PA
CBHW030747250426
43672CB00028B/1111